Positive Classroom Management Skills for School Librarians

Positive Classroom Management Skills for School Librarians

KAY BISHOP AND JENNY CAHALL

 **LIBRARIES UNLIMITED**

AN IMPRINT OF ABC-CLIO, LLC
Santa Barbara, California • Denver, Colorado • Oxford, England

Library of Congress Cataloging-in-Publication Data

Bishop, Kay, 1942–
    Positive classroom management skills for school librarians /
Kay Bishop, Jenny Cahall.
        p. cm.
    Includes bibliographical references and index.
    ISBN 978-1-59884-986-8 (pbk.) — ISBN 978-1-59884-987-5 (ebook)
1. School libraries—Administration.   2. School librarian-
student relationships.   3. Classroom management.   I. Cahall,
Jennifer.   II. Title.
    Z675.S3B565   2012
    025.1'978—dc23   2011033981

ISBN: 978-1-59884-986-8
EISBN: 978-1-59884-987-5

16 15 14 13 12   1 2 3 4 5

This book is also available on the World Wide Web as an eBook.
Visit www.abc-clio.com for details.

Libraries Unlimited
An Imprint of ABC-CLIO, LLC

ABC-CLIO, LLC
130 Cremona Drive, P.O. Box 1911
Santa Barbara, California 93116-1911

This book is printed on acid-free paper ∞

Manufactured in the United States of America

Contents

List of Figures   ix

Acknowledgments   xi

Introduction   xiii

Chapter 1   Positive School Librarian–Student Relationships   1
             Preventing Discipline Problems   2
             Correcting Student Behavior   4
             Following Up Discipline   6

Chapter 2   Lower Elementary Students   9
             Scheduling   10
             Gaining and Keeping Attention   10
             Rules and Procedures   13
             Storytimes   15
             Table Activities   17
             Transitions   19
             Dealing with Problem Children   21
             Rewards   22
             Working with Teachers, Support Staff,
                 and Parents   23
             Summary   24
             Scenarios   25

Chapter 3   Upper Elementary Students   27
             Scheduling   28
             Gaining and Keeping Attention   28

Rules and Procedures   29
Table Activities   30
Transitions   32
Dealing with Problem Children   33
Rewards   35
Working with Teachers, Support Staff,
      and Parents   36
Summary   38
Scenarios   38

Chapter 4   Middle School Students   39
Scheduling   40
Effective Communication   40
Rules and Procedures   41
Bullying   42
Class Activities   44
Dealing with Problem Students   45
Student Volunteers   46
Working with Teachers and Support Staff   47
Summary   50
Scenarios   50

Chapter 5   High School Students   51
Scheduling   52
Effective Communication   54
Rules and Procedures   55
Bullying   58
Class Activities   60
Dealing with Problem Students   61
Working with Teachers and Support Staff   62
Summary   63
Scenarios   64

Chapter 6   Students from Diverse Backgrounds   65
Effective Communication   67
Rules and Procedures   69
Bullying   69

	Class Activities	70
	Dealing with Problem Students	73
	Working with Teachers and Support Staff	73
	Summary	74
	Scenarios	74
Chapter 7	Technology	77
	Scheduling	77
	Effective Communication	78
	Rules and Procedures	78
	Class Activities	81
	Working with Teachers and Support Staff	83
	Summary	84
	Scenarios	85
Chapter 8	Library Design and Environment	87
	Overall Environment	87
	Facility Design and Layout	88
	Summary	93
	Scenarios	94
Works Cited		95
Index		97

List of Figures

2.1   Library Rules for Lower Elementary Students   13

2.2   Note to Parent or Guardian   24

3.1   Library Contract for Upper Elementary Students   35

3.2   Flyer to Parents or Guardians   37

4.1   Library Orientation Handout for Middle School Students   43

4.2   Collaborative Lesson Plan   48

5.1   Student Use of the School Library   53

5.2   Discipline Record   59

7.1   Signature Form for Internet Use   81

Acknowledgments

I would like to thank Edward Cummings, graduate assistant at the University at Buffalo, for research assistance, and the many school library media students at the University of Buffalo who during past years have shared with the author their observations of positive classroom management techniques of school librarians.

—Kay Bishop

Many thanks to Margaret Pence for her help with the graphics and to my family for their patience and support.

—Jenny Cahall

Introduction

The purpose of this book is to help school librarians prevent and deal with discipline problems that they may face when communicating with K–12 students. Though many of the author's current and former school library media students have shared that this is a major issue for them, the author (Dr. Kay Bishop) was unable to locate any book that specifically addresses this topic. Thus, she decided to write this much-needed book.

Positive management of students is emphasized throughout this book, with specific guidelines and strategies discussed in detail. Numerous examples drawn from the author's experiences as a school librarian and as a school library educator are included. All names of schools and librarians described in the examples have been changed, but they are based on real observations made by the author or by school library media students at the University of Buffalo.

The initial chapter deals with establishing positive relationships between school librarians and K–12 students. This chapter draws from general strategies used in classrooms, as well as techniques used by school librarians. Chapters 2, 3, 4, and 5 discuss characteristics of students in lower elementary grades, upper elementary grades, middle schools, and high schools and the numerous strategies that librarians can use to effectively manage these students in school libraries. Many specific examples are also presented. Chapter 6 addresses ways to communicate with diverse students, including students with special needs, and Chapter 7 discusses the management of students as they utilize technology in library settings. A final brief chapter addresses how to design school library facilities and environments to avoid potential discipline problems. All chapters, except the first one, conclude with summaries and scenarios that can be used for further discussion.

The intended audiences for the book are both pre-service and practicing school librarians. It is the sincere desire of the authors that both audiences find the information in the book beneficial as they communicate with and manage students in school library settings.

CHAPTER 1

Positive School Librarian–Student Relationships

Maintain a positive and enthusiastic attitude.

A positive attitude and enthusiasm are both contagious. School librarians who communicate positively with students and demonstrate a caring attitude and respect will generally have good relationships with students. Developing positive school librarian–student relationships is one of the most effective steps that can be taken to establish a good discipline environment in the school library. When students feel that they are respected, they are more likely to behave appropriately and show respect to those persons around them. Research shows that if the foundation of a good relationship is lacking, students will resist rules and procedures (Marzano 41).

By both demonstrating enthusiasm and making learning interesting, school librarians are able to more easily engage students. Scholars have noted that discipline works best when it is integrated with effective teaching practices (Curwin, Mendler, and Mendler 4). When students are actively engaged in enjoyable learning activities that are planned well and led by enthusiastic school librarians, there are apt to be few behavior problems.

While there are abundant articles about establishing good relationships between teachers and students, little has been written about building relationships between librarians and students. In 2000, Nancy

Thomas wrote an article in *School Library Media Activities Monthly* that looked at some of the library literature dealing with school librarian–student relationships. She noted that in 1982 Betty Martin was one of the first educators to call attention to the importance of the school librarian–student relationships, stating that librarians should "avoid interrupting, shaming, name calling, commanding, moralizing, lecturing, arguing, or criticizing" (56). Results from research dealing with the interrelationships of school librarians and students in the 1990s indicated a variety of reasons that serious attention should be paid to positive school librarian–student interactions (Thomas 39).

Many of the positive classroom management strategies and teacher–student interpersonal relationships advocated in education literature can be applied to school library settings. However, because circumstances may be different in school libraries than in classrooms (e.g., librarians may not know the names of all the students or the area of the library might be much larger than that of a classroom), it might be necessary to alter some techniques.

PREVENTING DISCIPLINE PROBLEMS

One of the most successful ways to prevent discipline problems is to establish rules and procedures early in the year. These rules and procedures should be discussed on the first class visit to the library. The printed rules should also be posted where they can easily be seen. Middle school and high school students often do not have regularly scheduled class visits to the library. In these cases, the school librarian should arrange with English teachers to bring their classes to the library for student orientations (perhaps in 6th grade for middle schools and in 9th grade for high schools). In an early visit to the library, the librarian should discuss with the students what the library can be used for and how it can help students throughout the school year.

Rules should be limited to those that are necessary to meet the expectations that all students can and will behave in an appropriate manner. Too many rules may challenge some students to find and do something that is not on the list (Gootman 41). The rules should be stated simply and positively and be age appropriate. It is likely that rules or procedures that are necessary for kindergarten students might be viewed as ridiculous in a high school library. Rules might also depend on school values and procedures. However, overall, rules should be designed to permit safe, enjoyable learning for everyone (Gootman 43).

When students know and follow procedures, such as where to return books or where to sit when they enter the library, there is less opportunity for disruptive behaviors. Having procedures or rituals for beginning and ending a class visit can be helpful. In the lower grades, a routine can be as simple as repeating an attention-getting jingle or singing a song at the beginning of a lesson. In high school, at the end of each class visit, the librarian might direct students to remain in their seats and wait for the bell before exiting the library, adding a reminder to push in chairs to keep pathways open as students exit.

Another effective prevention technique is to establish a library environment that supports and encourages appropriate academic and social behaviors by consistently recognizing and reinforcing desired behaviors. Praising students for their good behavior and providing many opportunities for students to be successful in their learning are two strategies that can be used successfully by school librarians. Again, the praise must be age appropriate. Older students may have different preferences for types of praise than do younger children. Regardless of the type of praise used, it should be directly linked to the behavior or skills that the librarian wishes to increase. Positive reinforcement points out good student behaviors, which the librarian wishes to see.

Setting high, but reasonable, expectations for both student behavior and achievement can also contribute to a positive school library environment. These expectations should be expressed clearly to students. For instance, before reading a book aloud to a kindergarten class, a librarian might say, "Because I am going to read this book to you today, all eyes now need to be on me. When I complete the story, we will then have time to ask questions and make comments about the story." Consequently, students know they are expected to look at the librarian and listen to the entire story without interrupting. Explanations of expectations should not be too lengthy, especially with young children.

Since most school librarians have a fairly limited amount of time with students, it is important to maximize routines in order to save time and create efficiency. For instance, having all materials ready when a class enters the library for a lesson, or using students to pass out materials, provides opportunities for the librarian to focus on the lesson and interact with students, rather than being diverted by time-consuming tasks. Student volunteers can also check out materials, shelve books, or collect hall passes at the circulation desk. Creating an environment where students have responsibilities can contribute to the prevention of behavior problems and help build a sense of community.

Maintaining proximity is another beneficial classroom management technique—whether it is seating a fidgety child close to the front at storytime or consistently walking about a room full of high school students who have gathered in the library before school. Moving toward a student who is initiating a problem or who is off-task is an effective strategy to prevent trouble from escalating. An experienced educator's look (intently staring at students who are starting to misbehave) can also silently communicate to the students that the librarian wishes the undesirable behavior to stop (Boynton and Boynton 38).

Having a basic knowledge of the students can help librarians manage library settings more effectively. For instance, being aware of which students may need to be watched more closely and which students can be left to quietly work independently can prevent potential problems. Librarians can seek the help of classroom teachers in getting to know more about students. In the same way, it is important for librarians to know their own libraries and the school. The awareness of one's surroundings sends out a tacit message that the librarian is in control and confident in his ability to manage students in the library.

Some schools have school-wide behavior policies or programs. These can be invaluable, as all students, teachers, and staff members are aware of expected behaviors. In many schools, these behaviors are visibly announced in signs throughout the schools: "At Brooks Elementary we respect ourselves, each other, and our environment," or "At Washington Middle School we are a family that works together through mutual respect and caring."

CORRECTING STUDENT BEHAVIOR

The goal of correcting student behavior is to encourage students to behave responsibly, not just be obedient to rules. Whenever possible, a student's behavior should be corrected in such a way as to maintain the dignity of the student. Embarrassing students or scolding them in front of their classmates not only will destroy a student's dignity, but also may lead to future behavior problems. Instead, it is important for students to have opportunities to provide input and make responsible decisions about their own behavior.

Misbehavior should be handled quickly and consistently. With young children, a time-out area may be needed; however, students should be allowed to reenter the group after an appropriate amount of penalty time. Inappropriate behavior with older students may require taking a student to an area away from other students and talking calmly about the library rule that was broken. Asking errant students, "What are you doing that is problematic?" or "Is what you are doing causing a problem?" gives students an opportunity to evaluate their behavior. When students are encouraged to reflect on their actions, they can then become more in control of those actions (Flicker and Hoffman 8). This method in itself may be enough to solve the discipline problem or serve as a first warning. Listening to students and showing interest in what is being said is essential. It is important to remember that interest is also conveyed by body language, such as good eye contact. If students are emotionally upset, it may help to reflect back the students' feelings in words, thus indicating to students that they are being heard. This does not mean that the librarian must agree with any and all feelings of the student, but it may help the student cope with the emotions and then work on solving the behavior problem.

Power struggles of any type between a librarian and student who is misbehaving should be avoided. A win-win resolution will be more likely to lead to improved student behavior in the future.

Any consequence that follows correcting misbehavior should be meaningful and related to the inappropriate behavior. The librarian may want to indicate to a student that she is disappointed that a consequence must be invoked and then communicate the expectation that the student will do better in the future. Consequences should make logical sense, help students become accountable for their actions, and keep the dignity of the student and librarian intact (Gootman 134).

A librarian might also recommend some alternative actions, suggesting, for example, "Instead of grabbing a book from Johnny's hand, next time perhaps you can ask Johnny if he will let you look at it when he is finished," or "Rather than trying to grab the book from Johnny, you could ask me to save the book for you when it is returned next week."

Whenever possible, a librarian should refrain from disciplining an entire class or group because of the misbehavior of one student. Group punishments are unfair to innocent students and tend to create animosity toward the librarian. If a particular behavior problem persists, it might be effective to create behavior contracts or plans with individual students. In any case, students should be involved in solving the problem and deciding on consequences for violating the contract or plan.

For more serious student behavior problems, such as intentionally inflicting harm on others, bullying, or repeatedly breaking rules, alternative measures must be taken. In those cases, the reasons for mis-behavior should be investigated before simply treating the symptoms. It is often necessary to involve teachers, school administrators, and parents in resolving serious discipline problems. Additionally, it is al-ways a good idea to document in writing any such occurrences, noting the names of possible witnesses to the incident.

Bullying is apt to have significant negative effects and, because it has become so common in our society, requires special attention. Ac-cording to the National Center for Educational Statistics, 27 percent of students reported being bullied in school in 2007 (*Bullying Statistics*). Bullying comes in various forms including teasing, spitting, pushing, and hitting. It can be either verbal or physical, with girl bullies tending to use verbal abuse, while more boys are involved in physical bullying. It is generally believed that students bully because bullying is a source of power; it is considered fun; or they believe that they are gaining peer approval by menacing others (Scarlett, Ponte, and Singh 93). It is a form of intimidation toward a student who is perceived as weaker in some way. Bullying may occur because of another student's race, re-ligion, sexual orientation, or disability. Sometimes it happens because the bully does not like or is jealous of the other person.

Educators have a responsibility to deal with bullying. In addition to providing good supervision throughout the school property, they should be proactive in educating students about the harms of bullying and intervene when bullying occurs. Research has indicated that high school teachers are less likely to intervene; thus, there is a need for sec-ondary teachers to be more vigilant and involved with this problem (Scarlett, Ponte, and Singh 93). All school librarians should be on the lookout for cases of bullying, not only in the library, but also through-out the school. Bullying must never be ignored and should be dealt with immediately. Librarians can be proactive in educating students and staff members about all kinds of bullying, including cyber bully-ing. Resources dealing with bullying should be easily accessible in the library. Additionally, librarians can volunteer to serve on school and community committees that address this serious problem.

FOLLOWING UP DISCIPLINE

Regardless of what strategy is used to administer discipline, it is al-ways a good idea to follow up with students. Young children need to be reassured that even though they may have been placed in time-out for disturbing other students during storytime, they can come back into the group, and that the librarian does not dislike them for their misbehavior. High school students who have lost library privileges for a week because of repeated broken rules need to know that when the week is ended, the librarian will welcome them with a pleasant, personal "Good morning" and a smile. All grudges should be dropped, and the student's original misbehavior must not be taken personally.

If a school librarian and student have made a contract to try to prevent misbehavior, then the librarian should have occasional formal or informal meetings to discuss how the contract is working. The same type of meetings should occur if a student is following a behavior plan. Sometimes it may be necessary to reevaluate the plan or make changes in the plan. Ideally, a contract or behavior plan is only needed for a limited amount of time, until the desired behavior is consistently achieved.

CHAPTER 2

Lower Elementary Students

Be prepared for the unexpected.

Young children can be full of surprises, and often those surprises come at unexpected times and places. Children in lower elementary grades are generally honest (sometimes brutally), and are not hesitant to express whatever is on their minds or whatever emotions they are feeling. In addition, these students have shorter attention spans than do older students and may have difficulty focusing on an activity. They often become quite fidgety when having to remain in one position for even short periods of time. Some of these younger students are very social and talkative, while others tend to be shy and need to learn to play and work with their peers. The shy students may also be hesitant to ask questions or seek advice. Since lower elementary students are just beginning to gain independence, they require much direction. They are also easily excited. The days before holidays or special school events may induce classes of students who are more difficult to manage than usual. Nonetheless, it is important to remember that students in the lower elementary grades respond well to caring authority and are very open to learning.

School librarians should understand these attributes of younger children when working with them. While some of these characteristics can make managing young children challenging, other characteristics contribute to delightful and rewarding experiences for both school librarians and students.

SCHEDULING

In elementary schools, there are often a variety of schedules, each of which will affect the management of students in a school library. If a school has a fixed schedule, which is often the case for the lower elementary classes, classes will come to the library for a specified period of time each week. This time period, again, may vary, but generally is approximately 30 minutes. In some schools, classes may visit the library only every other week. During the time spent in the library, students usually have a storytime or lesson, perhaps an activity at student tables, and a time for book selection and checkout. Classes are generally scheduled one after another, with teachers or paraprofessionals leading the students to the library, where they are dropped off and then picked up after the library time is complete. This frequently means that classes are arriving and leaving from the school library with little or no time in between, and with possible overlaps when teachers run late. Thus, dealing effectively with these students as they arrive and leave becomes an essential management task. This will be addressed in a later section entitled "Transitions."

Some school librarians have flexible scheduling for their lower elementary students. In flexible scheduling, students come to the library at various times throughout the week. Class visits are scheduled collaboratively between teachers and the librarian, while small groups of students or individual children come to the library when they need library resources. In flexible scheduling, a school librarian needs to possess not only the classroom management skills to deal with entire classes of students, but also knowledge of how to manage small groups of students.

Some schools use a combination of fixed and flexible scheduling for their school libraries. If a librarian meets with a class of students, plus at the same time also allows small groups of students or individual children to visit the library, then management of students becomes quite challenging. Having a library clerk or staff member who can assist students lessens the challenge; however, all library support persons should be well-trained in the management of students.

GAINING AND KEEPING ATTENTION

Because children in the lower elementary grades can be easily distracted and may have difficulty focusing on an activity, it is wise to have some techniques to gain and keep their attention. The following are some examples of how to accomplish this.

At Kendall Elementary School, the librarian greets the lower elementary grade classes at the beginning of each class period as the children enter the library. Often, the librarian addresses children by their names and directs them to sit on the floor near a rocking chair at the front of the storytime area, instructing a few children at a time to sit down on the carpeted floor before releasing the next group of students. Thus, there is a staggered arrival into the storytime area. The librarian walks toward the rocking chair and simply says, "Crisscross applesauce," and the children immediately sit on the floor with their legs crossed and hands in their lap.

At another school, a librarian uses the Give Me Five technique at the beginning of each class. This consists of repeating the following directions and utilizing accompanying hand motions:

- Eyes on the speaker (raises rounded fingers up to eyes to make glasses)
- Mouths closed (makes zipping motions across the lips)
- Hands raised (raises both hands in the air)
- Ears listening (places hands behind ears)
- Brain thinking (touches finger to one side of the head to indicate thinking)

Once the students get used to this technique, the librarian only needs to say the phrase "Give me five," and the children respond with the appropriate motions. If a child does not respond with the correct motions, the librarian reviews the rules individually and has the class practice them together.

Mr. Rodriguez, the librarian at Lincoln Elementary School, uses a raccoon puppet named Moody to come out after the children are seated and quiet in the library. If the class is noisy, Moody does not appear, and the students must wait until everyone is quiet. Moody is often then used during the library time to turn pages of the book that is being read or to react to the story. The students wait with anticipation for Moody to appear and participate in storytime.

At another elementary school, the librarian lights her "magic" (electric-powered) candle to indicate that storytime is about to begin, and the children become quiet immediately. At still another school, before opening a book to read, the librarian reminds the students of her expectations for their behavior: "Hands to yourself, eyes on the reader, listen while someone else is talking." She then tells the students that if these rules are not followed, she will need to stop reading.

If a school library serves preschool children, the following words can be spoken to help prepare the seated students for a listening activity.

- Open and shut them (open and shut raised hands)
- Open and shut them (open and shut raised hands again)
- Give a little clap (clap hands one time)
- Open and shut them (open and shut raised hands)
- Open and shut them (open and shut raised hands)
- Lay them in your lap (put both hands in lap)

At School #54, students enter the storytime area in the library where Ms. Kwaitowski, the school librarian, awaits them. After all students are seated, Ms. Kwaitowski brings out a special bag with a mystery item inside. She immediately has all the children's attention, and they are amazingly quiet. A few children are selected from the class to feel into the bag and try to guess what is inside. The surprise item is always related to the story that the librarian is going to share. When the article is revealed, Ms. Kwaitowski then provides an introduction to the book that she is preparing to read.

After student attention is initially gained, it may be necessary to establish attention again if children become noisy or fidgety. This is a time during which librarians can use positive reinforcement of good behavior: They might say, "I like that Jonny has his eyes on the book that we are reading and that Cassandra is listening quietly." Rather than giving attention to the students that are misbehaving, it may be more effective to focus attention on students who are behaving well.

At times when students are working on projects at library tables, a class as a whole might get too noisy. If the librarian needs to gain the attention of students, a "quiet sign" can be used. When a calm atmosphere is needed, the librarian might raise two fingers in a "V" formation; students, seeing the sign, begin making the quiet sign until the whole library is filled with students holding up the sign. Of course, such a technique must be taught to students early in the school year and used regularly. Clapping is another method frequently utilized to get students' attention. Sometimes, all teachers and support staff in a school use the same clapping pattern or quiet sign to gain the attention of students. Thus, after students learn the clapping pattern or quiet sign in the lower grades, the techniques can be employed anywhere in the school, including in the cafeteria or at an all-school assembly. These techniques seem to be particularly effective, as they are not directed at any one specific student and response is quick.

RULES AND PROCEDURES

Children need to know what type of behavior is appropriate in the school library. During the first visit to the library each year, the school librarian should explain both the rules and procedures that students are expected to follow. In an elementary school, rules should be kept to a minimum and should emphasize positive behaviors. They should also be simple, realistic, and set up to promote student success. Rules related to how to treat others should always be included. Posting the rules on a large laminated poster board in the library serves as a reminder to students. When a rule is broken, the librarian can bring the child's attention to the posted rules. It is important that all rules are consistently applied to all students. Figure 2.1 is a sample of a poster that could be used in an elementary school library.

Figure 2.1
Library Rules for Lower Elementary Students

LIBRARY RULES

✔ Listen carefully.
✔ Keep hands and feet to yourself.
✔ Respect school and personal property.
✔ Be kind to others.

Verona Elementary School Library

Students also need to know specific library procedures, such as where to go when they enter the library, how to check out books and other materials, where to place materials that are being returned to the library, and how to line up with a class to leave the library. Again, these procedures must be introduced or reviewed at the beginning of each school year. If new students enter the school during the year, they will also need to learn these procedures. A responsible student can be assigned to be a library buddy and assist such students.

Procedures vary greatly from school library to school library, depending on the scheduling of the library, the availability of clerical assistance, and the layout of the library. The following are some suggestions that can be utilized to help students follow the library procedures:

- Use signage in large print letters to indicate where materials are to be checked out and returned.
- Make an illustrated poster that demonstrates the procedure to check out materials.
- Tape a brightly colored line on the carpet along the path where students are to line up before leaving the library as a class.
- If using computerized checkout, provide an easy way for students to identify themselves (individual cards with their name, picture, ID number, and bar code printed on them). If photos are not available, children can decorate their cards with pictures that they will be able to identify.
- Use support staff or parent volunteers to assist young children with procedures.

Having consistent routines is also helpful in managing young students. For instance, the following routine could be used every time a class comes to the library:

1. Students enter the library and place their returned books on a cart that sits next to the entrance.
2. Students proceed to the storytime area, where they quietly seat themselves on the carpet.
3. After the storytime is finished, the librarian releases children in small groups to proceed to assigned places at tables.
4. After the table activity or lesson is completed, the librarian calls students from one table at a time to begin book selection.
5. When each student completes checking out a book, he then immediately proceeds to the lining-up space and sits on the floor, where he looks at or reads the materials that have been checked out.

Early in the academic year, these procedures should be taught and perhaps modeled by the librarian or selected students. Consistent following of routines will help children know where to go and what to do when visiting the library as a class.

STORYTIMES

In addition to some of the techniques that have been discussed, singing can be used to prepare children for storytime. The following lyrics can be sung at the beginning of each storytime for young children.

"Let's Get Ready for Storytime"

(sung to the tune of "Here We Go Round the Mulberry Bush")

We're all here for storytime,
Storytime, storytime.
We're all here for storytime.
Let's get ready now.

Can you turn your ears up high, (tweak ears)
Ears up high, ears up high?
Can you turn your ears up high
So that you can hear?

Can you open your eyes up wide, (point to eyes)
Eyes up wide, eyes up wide?
Can you open your eyes up wide
So that you can see?

Now we're ready for storytime, (clap)
Storytime, storytime.
Now we're ready for storytime.
Let's get started now.

In one school library where the children tend to get fidgety during storytime and move out of their personal spaces, the librarian uses a unique method.

After the kindergarten students are seated for storytime, Ms. Morris hands each child a plastic egg and talks to the class about how a mother animal has to be careful with her eggs to keep her babies safe. In order to do the same with their eggs, the children are asked to sit still and keep the eggs on their laps. She reminds them that if they wiggle too much or move the eggs about, their babies will roll off their laps and won't be safe. During storytime, Ms. Morris occasionally makes a visual check and asks students how their eggs are doing. This serves as a gentle reminder to any children who are getting fidgety. Ms. Morris's management technique is introduced early in the school year after she reads the children *The Egg Story* by Anca Hariton. Then each time the children come to storytime, they are handed their plastic eggs to keep safe.

Using thoughtful care in the seating of children for storytime can lessen potential behavior problems. If students are seated on the floor in a carpeted area, the seating area should provide adequate space between each child. Obtaining sample squares from a carpet store and placing them where the librarian wants children to sit is one way to obtain enough space between children and at the same time add some color to the area. Having an assigned seat for storytime may be necessary if children are consistently unruly and bothering students sitting close to them. Another possible solution is to ask the classroom teacher to line up children so students are not next to someone with whom potential behavior problems might occur. Then, as the children enter the library, the librarian instructs them to stay in the correct order as they are seated in the storytime area. Small chairs for younger students are also used in some library settings. If chairs are the preferred or only possible seating, they should be set up ahead of time with adequate space between each chair and the lines of chairs staggered, to provide visibility for the children.

All children want to be able to see the illustrations in the book that is being read aloud. If they are unable to see, they will most likely start moving out of place or will interrupt the story by announcing loudly that they cannot see. When reading books out loud, the librarian must remember to show all children the pages that are illustrated. In addition to having a good seating pattern for the students, it is also important for the school librarian to select appropriate books to read aloud. Books selected for storytime should have large, brightly colored illustrations. If a librarian is particularly fond of a book that does not have illustrations large enough to be shared by an entire class, the librarian can consider telling the story (perhaps using a puppet to narrate the story) or purchasing the book in a DVD format, rather than reading it aloud.

Young children, particularly pre-school and kindergarten students, tend to interrupt a reader who is sharing a book out loud. The children may want to talk about something in the story, ask a question, or say something that is totally unrelated to the story, such as, "My mother made me eat oatmeal for breakfast and I hate oatmeal!" To reduce the occurrence of such interruptions, it is a good idea to remind students to wait until the story is finished before asking questions or making comments.

> Mrs. Gonzalez, a school librarian at Willard Elementary School, developed a technique to prevent interruptions, such as "My Uncle Joe has a dog that looks like that," or "My mother's name is Maria, too." Mrs. Gonzalez purchased a plastic crown at a local party supply store. Before each storytime, she places the crown and a book that she is planning to share with the children on a cart. At the beginning of storytime, she then asks a student to retrieve the book and crown. When she places the crown on her head, the students automatically know that no one is supposed to interrupt the story. When Mrs. Gonzalez is finished reading the story and has completed her lesson, she then removes the crown from her head. This is the signal that students can begin to comment on the story, ask questions, or share personal anecdotes.

Some librarians ask children if they have anything to share before beginning the storytime. Students may then share aloud news or observations. Of course, there is the risk that such sharing may go on for a longer period than desired or that something may be shared that the librarian is not prepared to deal with—"My daddy yelled at my mom this morning, and she told him to get out of the house, and I am feeling really sad." When librarians want the sharing time to end, they can redirect the students' focus and say, "Now that we have shared our news, we are ready to sit still and listen to a wonderful story."

Because young children have short attention spans, it is wise to plan to read or tell a relatively short story during storytime. In first and second grades, the stories can begin to get more lengthy and complex. Other activities such as songs, poems, or stretching and movements can be interspersed if more than one book is being read.

TABLE ACTIVITIES

In some libraries, lower elementary students participate in activities at library tables. Seating may be random or there may be assigned seats.

In the St. Joseph Elementary School Library, there are several round student tables. Sister Cravey, the school librarian, places a different animal picture in the middle of each table. As children enter the library, Sister Cravey randomly hands them a book marker with an animal picture on it. Students then proceed to the table that has the matching animal on it. The randomization makes it possible to break up any cliques that have formed in the classroom. It also gives students opportunities to work with a variety of other children during group library projects or lessons.

If children object to the assigned seating being used for each library visit, the librarian can explain to the students that their classroom teachers have only one class of students to remember and work with, but a school librarian must learn the names of every student in the school. Thus, a seating chart for every class is very helpful to the librarian.

When students are expected to immediately begin an activity that requires materials of some type, then all materials (paper, crayons, and pencils) should be placed on the tables where children will be seated before the class arrives. However, if students are first listening to a story or being taught a lesson, then placing such materials on the table will most likely tempt children to begin fidgeting with them. In such cases, materials can be arranged and placed in some other place in the library, for instance on a movable cart. One or two responsible student helpers can then be selected to help pass out the materials. When the activity is completed, these same students or other student helpers can then pick up the materials and return them to the cart. It also works to have one student from each table pass out and return materials; however, it is best not to have too many students transporting materials simultaneously, as this may become noisy and disruptive.

Some librarians like to set up learning centers at tables in their school libraries. Again, all materials should be in place at each center before students arrive. Children are then instructed to move from one center to another, making crafts, completing word searches, assembling puzzles, playing educational games, or any of a variety of possible activities. School librarians using such centers need to be prepared for a relatively noisy environment as children move from one center to another and express their enthusiasm about or frustrations with the activities in the centers. It may be necessary at times to use the library quiet sign or clapping pattern to reduce the level of noise. However, if a librarian is willing to prepare creative learning centers and to manage such an environment, the reward is great—children who have fun while learning and who eagerly look forward to their library visits.

TRANSITIONS

In addition to gaining and keeping attention, effectively moving lower elementary students from one area to another is probably one of the most challenging tasks for new school librarians. Fortunately, there are many good techniques that can be used to help do this. Observing other educators' methods is one of the best ways to learn what works well.

Librarians always hope that lower elementary students will arrive at the entrance to the library in an orderly manner. If this is not the case, then the librarian should make certain that the students are lined up and quiet before entering the library. This may entail taking a few minutes in the hallway to remind students of library rules and expectations. Once students are quiet and ready to listen to directions, the librarian can then begin transitioning the students to the library area where the first activity is going to take place. This is accomplished by having a few students at a time move to the desired location.

At other times during a class visit to the library, students might also be expected to move from one area to another (for instance, from the storytime area to activity tables or from tables to book shelves for book selection). This can be accomplished effectively by releasing a few children at a time. The librarian can ask students who are wearing apparel of a certain color to leave in one group and then call out another color, and then another, until all students have moved to the new area of the library. Some other grouping categories that can be used for this technique are:

- students wearing certain types of shoes (sandals, sneakers, boots)
- students whose birthdays are in particular months
- students whose first names begin with a chosen letter
- students who walk to school, ride a bus, or are picked up in a car
- students who have brown eyes, green eyes, or blue eyes.

Some librarians reward good student behavior when deciding which children will be released first for book selection or lining up to leave the library.

Mrs. Sotar, the school librarian at John F. Kennedy Elementary School, has a beautiful gold, sparkly magic wand that she uses to help transition kindergarten students from one area of the library to another. After storytime is complete, Mrs. Sotar uses her magic wand and taps the shoulders of students who have listened well and remembered to raise their hands to speak during sharing time. Children who are tapped with the magic dust are then able to make their way to the tables where Mrs. Sotar has laid out a large collection of books that are available for checkout. When the majority of students from the first group have made selections, she then taps the shoulders of more students, which is the indication that it is their turn to make selections. Mrs. Sotar either talks with the students who are waiting their turns or sings songs with them. Volunteer parents assist as children make their book selections, check them out, and sit in a line on the floor to look at their books. By scheduling all four kindergarten classes on the same morning, Mrs. Sotar is able to have one or more volunteers available on the day when they are most needed.

Another librarian transitions kindergarten and first graders by lining up the students and then having them walk behind her across the library, as she sings the following song:

Here comes the train,
Here comes the train,
Coming down the track,
Here comes the train,
Here comes the train,
Stopping on the track.

This technique provides an orderly routine for moving from one area to another, and the children know to stop when the song ends.

Mr. Geair, the librarian at Perkins Primary School, is very musical and frequently uses songs to provide positive behavior reinforcement as students move about the library. He sings, "Looking for books, looking for books; I see Jenny and Matthew finding their books" or "Checking out books, checking out books; Michael and Sebastian are checking out books." Children quietly listen and move about the library, listening to hear if their names will be used in his song. Students who are off task quickly move to appropriate areas in hopes of being added to the song. Mr. Geair often changes the tunes and lyrics of his songs or uses an instrumental accompaniment, and the students wait eagerly to hear what he will sing each week.

Young students should line up in an orderly fashion to leave the library and return to their classrooms. Table numbers can be called to accomplish this or children can be directed to sit down in a line in a designated area when they have completed their book checkout.

At those times, a teacher or paraprofessional may be late and children from their class are lined up and ready to leave. It is at such times that school librarians will be thankful that they possess a large repertoire of songs, rhymes, and poems to share with the younger students. Sometimes making simple statements to which the students can respond with motions can keep children occupied until the teacher arrives. "Raise your right hand if you saw the movie *Toy Story 3* this past weekend" or "Hop with your left foot if you ate taco salad for lunch in the cafeteria." Playing Simple Simon with book parts also works. "Simple Simon says to touch the spine of your library book," or "Simple Simon says to touch the front cover of your book."

DEALING WITH PROBLEM CHILDREN

Problem students exist at all grade levels. Often, young children who are considered to be problematic in an elementary school may simply not be as behaviorally mature as their peers. If a child's behavior (for instance, laying down instead of sitting in crisscross fashion during a story) is not bothering other children, then it might be more effective to use selective ignoring, rather than interrupting a lesson to remind the child of the appropriate position. However, sometimes a young child consistently exhibits unacceptable behavior that is disturbing or harmful to others. In such instances, the librarian must respond quickly and deal with the child calmly. For instance, a child who every week pinches students who sit close by during storytime should be moved away from other children. Directing the child to move to a position next to the librarian may solve the problem, since the librarian can then monitor the child's behavior more easily. If unacceptable behavior continues, a time-out may be necessary. It should be executed calmly and with as little interruption to the story or lesson as possible. It is best to place a time-out area or chair behind the students, but still in eyesight of the librarian, not only because the librarian is able to see the child, but also because the child can still participate in the activity and is not totally isolated from the class.

REWARDS

Some school librarians use rewards as a strategy when working with children. These librarians like to use rewards that motivate good behavior for an entire class.

As the children in Lowell Elementary School enter the library, Mr. Dean, the librarian, brings out Library Mouse, a hand puppet used for a variety of student reminders. When all students are in their assigned seats at tables, Library Mouse comes alive. If Mr. Dean rubs one side of Library Mouse's whiskers, the students know they have entered the library quietly. If he rubs the other side, then the students know they are sitting properly. If Library Mouse's tail begins to swing, then the children realize that all students in the class returned their books on time. If Library Mouse performs all three actions, then the class gets a check mark on a large poster that hangs on the wall. The class with the most checks at the end of the year receives a yummy ice cream sundae party.

Other possible rewards for the entire class are giving a sticker to each child when all students listen quietly to a story or providing special opportunities for each child to select a treasure from a treasure chest if all students in a class have good behavior in the library for four weeks in a row. Sometimes, rewards are given for a combination of group and individual efforts. This is the case in the following:

Ms. Flynn, the librarian at Ogelby Elementary School, uses marbles as a management and reward technique. She has a large glass jar for each class. After students from a class are seated, the librarian looks at the students at each table. She then hands a marble to a student at a table where all students are quiet and asks that student to place the marble in the class jar. She proceeds on to each table where all students are sitting quietly. If the children at all six tables are quiet when they are seated, then Ms. Flynn places an additional marble into the jar. Individuals can also earn extra marbles for the class during the library time. If a student proves to be an outstanding role model for peers by helping or otherwise positively contributing to the library experience, that child is given a marble and can place it in the jar. When the class jar is filled with marbles, each student gets to select a prize from a prize box. The jar is then emptied, and the class has an opportunity to fill it again.

Some school librarians and classroom teachers do not believe in the philosophy of giving rewards. This is fine. In any educational setting, plenty of verbal praise, in place of prizes, can promote good student behavior and establish a positive learning environment.

WORKING WITH TEACHERS, SUPPORT STAFF, AND PARENTS

Collaboration with teachers, support staff, and parents is especially important in the lower elementary grades. Frequently, classroom teachers work with thematic units. A school librarian can enrich the curriculum and actively engage students by selecting materials for storytime that relate to the theme that is being featured in a classroom. Consultation with classroom teachers is also important for any problem children. If a teacher is using a particular management technique to improve the behavior of a child in the classroom, it is helpful for the school librarian to consistently apply the same technique, if possible.

Often, paraprofessionals work with classroom teachers in the lower elementary classes. Sometimes, these support staff also accompany a class to the library. Thus, it is important for such staff members to be aware of library procedures and rules. Many paraprofessionals are also willing to help with table activities, such as craft projects. The presence of an additional adult can be particularly helpful if a young child needs to leave the library to go to the bathroom. School librarians who are fortunate enough to have full- or part-time clerks in their libraries should spend time training their clerks, not only in library procedures such as checking out books, but also in positive techniques that can be used to effectively manage and assist students.

Parents are often more involved in school activities with their younger children than with secondary students. Many parents, guardians, and grandparents are willing to assist in some manner in elementary school settings. There are no better advocates for a school library than parents; thus, inviting parents into the library as volunteers can reap many benefits for a library. If volunteers see that materials are old and should be replaced, or that a clerk is needed to assist the librarian, they often will take action to help remedy the situation. It is important for school librarians to create positive parent attitudes about the school library and the librarian's relationships with their children. One simple way to help do this is by letting parents know when their children have demonstrated good behavior in the library. The form in Figure 2.2 can be quickly filled out and handed to a classroom teacher at the end of a library period, with a request that the form be placed in the child's

Figure 2.2
Note to Parent or Guardian

Just Thought You Would Like to Know

_____ showed great behavior today in the library by:

(Student Name)

☐ Listening quietly to a story

☐ Remembering to raise a hand before talking during sharing time

☐ Reminding a friend about library procedures

☐ Saying thank you after being helped by the librarian

Other: _____

_____

_____

Date: _____

School Librarian: _____

Taylor Elementary School Library

---

backpack or folder that goes home with the child. Sending home just one or two such notes during a day can begin to establish positive relationships with parents or guardians.

SUMMARY

Having an understanding of the typical characteristics exhibited by children in the lower grades can be helpful to school librarians as they manage student behavior and activities in the library. School librarians can learn and utilize many techniques to help them gain and keep students' attention and transition students from one area of the library to another, two of the greatest challenges in dealing with younger children. Rules and procedures must also be carefully explained to lower elementary students. Additionally, librarians should deal calmly and quickly with consistently inappropriate student behavior problems. With the assistance of other school personnel and parents, school librarians can successfully manage young students in positive school library environments.

SCENARIOS

Think about or discuss how you could handle the following situations:

1. You are a school librarian in an elementary school. When Mrs. Jordan's first-grade class comes to the library for storytime, six-year-old Lily cannot seem to pay attention to the story. She pushes the students who sit next to her and constantly tries to get their attention.

2. You are a school librarian in an elementary school. It is the beginning of the year and you are meeting with Ms. Rinehart's kindergarten class for the first time. Mitchell interrupts you during the story you are reading to the class, and with tears in his eyes loudly announces, "I have to pee, right now." There is no other adult present in the library, and there is no bathroom in the library.

3. You are a school librarian in an elementary school where one second-grade class arrives very noisily at the library entrance every week. The students do not stay in line, and they push each other as they attempt to be the first student in line.

CHAPTER 3

Upper Elementary Students

Keep rules to a minimum and be consistent in enforcing them.

Children in the upper elementary grades can easily understand rules and follow them. In fact, they often have a special interest in rules and rituals. Upper elementary students are beginning to become independent learners and most can stay on task for at least 20–30 minutes. However, some children in grades 3–5 tend to daydream. Upper elementary students like to learn by doing and by making connections. They also learn best in environments where acceptance and belonging are encouraged. Most children in the upper elementary grades are proud of academic achievements. These students often enjoy group activities and playing on teams, but close friendships are generally with persons of the same sex. Children in grades 3–5 are usually energetic, friendly, and have a good sense of humor. Many of these students are voracious readers and enjoy reading about characters their age from the past, present, or future. They do not always see things as black or white and are beginning to see the motivation behind behaviors. Many of these children like to collect things, but their interests change frequently (North American Montessori Center).

School librarians find that upper elementary students are generally easy to manage in a school library setting. These students are able to concentrate on lessons and work well on group projects. Upper elementary children may look to the school librarian for reader advisement, and they also enjoy listening to chapters of books that are read aloud to them. Thus, school librarians can plan an abundance of activities that motivate upper elementary students to read and to learn information literacy skills.

SCHEDULING

Some elementary schools use flexible scheduling for their school libraries. In those cases, students arrive in small groups, with the librarian determining the size of the group that can be sent from any one classroom. The size allowed may depend on the size of the library and available seating, as well as whether there is library support staff to assist with the management of students. In addition to small groups, teachers can schedule their entire class for library lessons or check-out at various times, but are then generally required to remain with the students. Schools using flexible scheduling have the advantage of having at least two adults present to plan and implement library lessons, as well as to manage students.

Fixed scheduling, in which whole classes come to the library (usually without teachers remaining in the library), is common in elementary schools. In some schools, there is a mixture of flexible and fixed library scheduling. Most often in those cases, upper elementary students are flexibly scheduled, while the lower grades have fixed schedules each week. Whether a library is on a flexible, fixed, or mixed schedule is sometimes determined by the school district, but almost as often by individual schools.

In schools where upper elementary students are on flexible schedules, the librarian must learn to manage groups of different grade levels, often while there is an entire class present in the library for a lesson. Some teachers take undue advantage of flexible scheduling by frequently sending problem students to the library simply to remove the students from their classrooms for long periods of time. A librarian may need to meet with a classroom teacher to help remedy such a situation.

GAINING AND KEEPING ATTENTION

One of the best ways to gain and keep the attention of upper elementary students is to warmly welcome them when they enter the library, making eye contact with the students and addressing them by name. Providing a class an introduction on how they are going to spend their time in the library gives the children direction and focus. Using a calm voice throughout a lesson also has a settling effect on the students. A simple 5, 4, 3, 2, 1 countdown method can be used to obtain children's attention when needed.

> Mrs. Baldwin, the school librarian at Elmore Elementary School, gains the attention of upper elementary students by posting a puzzle on the whiteboard before each library visit. When the students arrive at the library and take their seats, they immediately spend the first few minutes trying to solve the puzzle. The brief amount of time devoted to this activity allows the children to make a transition to the library environment in a creative and orderly manner. Mrs. Baldwin is able to engage the students' attention and direct it in a positive manner to keep students occupied so inappropriate behavior does not have time to blossom.

Asking questions that require critical thinking makes students active participants in lessons and helps keep them engaged. Reflecting positively on each student's answer, even if it is wrong, will make students feel comfortable. Some possible comments include, "You are on the right track," or "I can see why you might think that." If a student goes off task, the librarian can simply state the child's name, and this is often enough to pull the child back in without stopping the lesson or drawing attention to bad behavior.

Upper elementary children are still eager to answer questions, in stark comparison to many middle and high school students. Thus, it is a good idea to ask students to raise their hands when they are ready to respond to a question. It is not necessary for the librarian to acknowledge every raised hand, but different students should be called upon during a lesson to give as many students as possible an opportunity to participate. Each student answer should be acknowledged before moving on to another raised hand.

RULES AND PROCEDURES

It is best to keep identical rules in the library for all students in grades K-5. These rules should be easily understood and kept to a minimum. Upper elementary students are quick to recognize teachers who play favorites or who let rules slide; thus, consistency is paramount.

By the time students reach the upper elementary grades, they are familiar with library procedures and the care of library materials. Thus, generally a great deal of time does not need to be spent on these topics. However, a quick review at the beginning of the school year is a good idea and will provide guidance to any new students in the school. Many students in the upper elementary grades are able to assist a school librarian with procedures, such as checking in and out materials and putting books in appropriate places on the shelves.

Librarians should also provide clear directions to students regarding the procedures to follow if a fire drill or lock-down occurs while they are in the library. In such an event, the librarian should remain calm, with the intention that students will mimic that calmness. After a fire drill, librarians should thank students for doing a good job. While the incident is fresh in the minds of the students, they should review the procedures that were followed.

Upper elementary students can be taught how to use the library automation system and barcode scanner so they are able to check out their own books. The advantages of this are that students are able to independently use their library cards, and the librarian has time to provide reading guidance to students. With well-designed rules and procedures, school librarians will find that they can look forward to productive and organized library visits from students in the upper elementary grades.

TABLE ACTIVITIES

School librarians need to integrate interesting and age appropriate activities into their library lessons. Doing so will make it possible for a librarian to manage students effectively. Often, for upper elementary students these activities take place at tables in the library, where students have opportunities to interact with other students. If time permits, before students enter the library, the librarian should place all the lesson materials on the tables. If scheduling does not permit this task and no other adult helpers are present in the library, then the librarian can select a student from each table to pass out and collect materials. Some librarians also keep student folders for each class and place them in separate crates. The folders contain library materials, along with pencils. In this way, students never forget their folders, their work from the previous week, or a writing utensil.

Although seating at tables has some advantages for group work, it also can be challenging for managing a class. After students are seated, the librarian should clearly communicate expectations for student behavior and work habits. If those expectations are not met, a librarian needs to consider management techniques, such as the following:

Ms. Sage, the librarian at Willard Elementary School, teaches information literacy skills to upper elementary students by having them work on a variety of group projects. In one instance, four boys sitting at the same table were noisy and did not get on task after a project had been explained to the class. Ms. Sage asked Michael, one of the boys, if he would be her helper for the day by turning the lights on and off when she needed to gain the students' attention. Michael was happy to be chosen for this task, and was only slightly disappointed when the librarian moved his seat to another table that was closer to the lights. With the group dynamic disrupted, the other boys settled down and began working on their project. Making this preemptive move to avoid a potentially disruptive situation and doing it so the student felt valued, instead of punished, worked well.

Sometimes, providing choices to students who are misbehaving can solve a problem. For instance, if two students continuously talk and distract others, the librarian can ask, "Are you going to sit quietly or should you choose a different place to sit?" Letting the students make the decision to move encourages them to make wise choices. Any time that a librarian can change a punishment (such as moving a student away from friends) to an independent decision to behave well, it is a good strategy. If the student chooses to sit elsewhere, it also presents an opportunity for the librarian to unobtrusively praise the student for good decision-making.

When students lose focus, a school librarian can give them gentle reminders or ask them questions to draw their attention back to their task. Sometimes a rhetorical question, such as, "Should we be talking about TV shows right now?" can act as a quick reminder of expected behaviors. If noise levels get too high during group projects, a librarian can also utilize a series of claps that students are expected to repeat while immediately becoming quiet. At the end of a lesson, a librarian should review with the children what they have learned. Students should be asked to connect their learning to ideas that were discussed in previous weeks. This will help make the library a productive learning place.

Establishing a predictable library routine with each class assists with classroom management. While lessons and activities may change, the basic routine that students follow should be the same for each library visit. This consistency will help students successfully complete tasks.

TRANSITIONS

In most cases, upper elementary students who are making a class visit to the library will need to move from one part of the library to another part. Thus, it becomes necessary to manage students in ways that make it possible to do this in an orderly fashion.

At the Hitchcock Intermediate School Library, there are six tables at which upper elementary students sit when they enter the library. Each student sits at an assigned seat at one of the tables. The tables are named after popular upper elementary series books, such as the Harry Potter table or the Chronicles of Narnia table. The assigned tables make it possible for the librarian to maintain control over the students when they are required to move around the library. When it is time for students to browse for books, to check out materials, or to line up to return to the classroom, the librarian looks for a table where students are sitting quietly and calls that table first, using the table name. This simple technique helps students remember their assigned seats in the library and transitions students in a quiet and organized manner.

At another school, as students enter the library, they blindly select a colored dot from a bag of dots. The children choose a seat at the table where their dot matches the color of a pencil box. The students enjoy the opportunity to select their seats and also wait eagerly to see who will be sitting at their table.

Students in the upper elementary grades usually have a transition period when they begin to check out books. If students are working independently, the librarian can instruct them to begin browsing for books when they have completed their library assignment, or can call the names of tables if students are participating in group projects. The browsing and check-out period also has potential to create a noise challenge; gaining the students' attention may then become necessary. In one elementary school, the librarian uses the following unusual technique:

When Mr. Yang wants the students' attention, he simply says, "SALAMI." It is said with calmness, but in a very serious tone. After hearing this signal, students are expected to stop (S) and look (AL) at me (AM) immediately (I). If Mr. Yang hears talking or sees movement after saying the acronym, he tells the students that this is unacceptable and asks them if they can improve their response before he says the acronym again. He praises the class for good results. This method works well with upper elementary students because it incorporates fun into class management. It is a successful technique because the librarian uses it sparingly, and thus it has an impact.

In some libraries, students are not allowed to check out additional books if they have not returned materials that are already checked out. It is essential that these students are kept busy during check-out time. They should be allowed to read magazines, work on word search or maze activities, or simply browse through high-interest reference materials, such as *The Guinness Book of World Records.* Another alternative is to ask the students to help with an activity, such as selecting books for younger children who will be visiting the library later in the day. The best solution is not to limit students from checking other materials, but to remind them to return any missing items the next day.

From time to time, a librarian might have lined up students to return to the classroom after a library visit, and yet the classroom teacher is late coming to retrieve the students. Upper elementary students enjoy riddles and jokes, so have a few ready to tell when this happens to maintain the students' attention and make it less likely that a few unstructured moments develop into disruptive student behavior. Short games relating to books can also serve this purpose. For instance, the students can play "Stump the Librarian" and ask a question about a book or an author to see if the librarian can guess what book or author is being described. The librarian can also have an envelope of charade items that can be acted out while they wait for their teacher's arrival.

DEALING WITH PROBLEM CHILDREN

Problem children can be present at any grade level. However, dealing with a problem student in the upper elementary grade level requires prompt action to make it clear that the behavior that is being exhibited is not acceptable. This must be done as unobtrusively as possible and without humiliating the student.

Mr. Joslin, the school librarian at Washington Elementary School, is particularly good at dealing with problem children in a calm, but effective manner. If a child is misbehaving during a lesson, instead of singling out the student, he moves physically closer to the child and continues with the lesson. However, at one point during a class lesson, a third-grade student became extremely disruptive and began running around the library and knocking books from the shelves. Without interrupting his lesson, Mr. Joslin gently put his hand on the student's shoulder, led him out the doorway, and pointed him down the hallway towards his classroom. Mr. Joslin was then able to wrap up the lesson and allow students to look for books as he picked up the phone and called the classroom teacher to let her know that the student was on his way back to the classroom.

If an upper elementary student continually displays disruptive behavior in the library, the librarian can suggest the use of a contract that is developed between the student and librarian. The contract reminds the student of the particular behavior that needs to be improved. For instance, if a student calls out answers continually without raising his hand, this could be the goal that is addressed in the contract. When such a contract is developed in elementary school, parents and the classroom teacher should be informed. It is also recommended that a parent signature be on the contract.

There will be times when a contract does not work, and another strategy must be tried. Some problem students exhibit antisocial behaviors, which is a topic that has been studied by researchers in recent years. Behavior management that works with typical students frequently does not work with antisocial students. The older these students get, the more serious their problems become, and the more difficult they are to manage. These students have sometimes been diagnosed with oppositional defiant disorders or conduct disorders and are in need of special interventions (Walker, Ramsey, and Gresham 8–10). Librarians should be aware of any individualized educational programs (IEPs) or behavior management plans that are in effect for such students. They should work cooperatively with classroom teachers and parents since IEPS and behavior management plans also need to be followed when children are in the library.

Parents or guardians generally have the most influence in their children's lives. Thus, librarians and teachers must work as partners with parents to address concerns about problem students. Pooling knowledge about a child and working together can be the best way to find a solution for serious behavior problems. The first step in finding such a solution is to calmly listen to the parents describe the child's life outside of school. It is important that all adults involved feel that they are on an equal footing, and all have the same positive intentions for the child (Gootman 13–16).

School librarians can contribute to the education of problem students by encouraging the children to meet appropriate behavior expectations. Helping these students become academically successful will usually also contribute positively to the behavior of the students.

Figure 3.1
Library Contract for Upper Elementary Students

Dayton Elementary School

Library Contract

Date _____

_____ promises to

_____

If student does as agreed, then student will

_____

If student does *not* do as agreed, then student will

_____

This contract will be in effect for

_____

_____   _____
Student signature   Teacher signature

_____
Parent signature

REWARDS

Some librarians like to use points or chips to reward students for being responsible with library materials and for displaying appropriate behavior. These points or chips can be redeemed for prizes (bookmarks, stickers, or paperback books) or special privileges, such as serving as a library volunteer or eating lunch with the librarian. Although individual rewards are used less often in upper elementary grades than with younger students, several librarians like to use class-wide rewards for students in grades 3–5.

> At School #23, Ms. Higgins, the school librarian, likes to use a point system for the students' awareness and other skills demonstrated during their scheduled library visits. The students earn one point when everyone in the class is an active participant in the lesson, one point if all students return their books, one point if all children are good listeners, and one point if the group table is clean (no papers on it and all chairs pushed in) at the end of the library visit. The class that earns the most points during the year is rewarded with a party of their choice, ice cream sundaes or pizza. The students take the point system seriously and are excited to report back to their classroom teacher the number of points they earned after each library lesson.

In a few schools, students receive grades for their academic accomplishments and behavior in the library. Some librarians, however, view grading as detrimental and prefer to have students obtain information literacy skills for the intrinsic reward of learning. They also value positive relationships with students that are independent of grades.

WORKING WITH TEACHERS, SUPPORT STAFF, AND PARENTS

Librarians who use flexible scheduling have a unique opportunity to collaborate with classroom teachers to plan and implement library lessons that relate to the topics being studied in the classroom. During their preparation periods, teachers are able to meet with the librarian and discuss possible lessons, including the objectives, materials that will be needed, activities, and assessment of the lesson. This is also an ideal time for classroom teachers to share information about particular students: for instance, those who may have IEPs or those who might need alternative formats of a lesson. The individual and shared responsibilities of the teacher and librarian should also be addressed in a written lesson plan.

It is more difficult to find available times to meet with teachers when a fixed library schedule is utilized in a school. However, in such cases, a librarian can still coordinate library lessons with classroom teachers through e-mail messages or by attending grade-level planning meetings.

Support staff can be extremely valuable to a school library and to the students using the library. Clerical duties, such as checking out and processing books, can be assigned to a support staff member. In addition, support staff can be trained to help manage students. Unfortunately, in many schools, full-time library support personnel are not available to assist with such duties, and the librarian must assume many of the clerical duties, thus leaving less time to positively interact with students.

In many schools, it is possible to obtain volunteer assistance from parents, grandparents, or guardians. Depending on their backgrounds and interests, volunteers can perform a variety of tasks. Often, volunteers enjoy working directly with the students, so they should be oriented to the library rules and procedures, as well as to the discipline expectations.

All parents and guardians should receive flyers relating to library procedures and events. In addition, the librarian should create a school library Web site where parents can obtain information about the students' activities in the library. Figure 3.2 is a sample flyer that could be sent home to parents.

Figure 3.2
Flyer to Parents or Guardians

Please help your child remember that the last day to return all library books is June 16.

Don't FORGET!

SUMMARY

Elementary schools vary on how their upper-level students are scheduled to visit the library. Thus, school librarians must be flexible in the management of these students and be proficient in working with relatively large classes of students, as well as with small groups of students who come into the library for a variety of purposes. Upper level elementary students are able to easily understand and follow library rules and procedures. However, any misbehavior should be addressed quickly and consistently. If early intervention in the lower grades has not occurred with some students, behavior problems are likely to increase. In those cases, school librarians need to work cooperatively with classroom teachers, parents, and guardians.

SCENARIOS

Think about or discuss how you could handle the following situations:

1. You are a school librarian in an elementary school that uses flexible scheduling. When teachers schedule a class into the library, they are required to accompany the class and work collaboratively with the librarian. One fifth-grade teacher often brings her class to the library, but pays little attention to the class, ignoring students who are kicking other students, throwing books, and generally horsing around.

2. You are a school librarian in an elementary school that has flexible scheduling. Joey and Zack are third-grade boys who frequently come to the library together from Ms. Halliday's class. They are constantly pushing each other and being disruptive while in the library.

3. You are a librarian in an elementary school that uses mixed scheduling, with the lower grades having fixed times in the library and the upper grades coming to the library on a flexible basis. While this schedule worked well last year when you had a full-time clerk, the clerk's hours have been reduced to half time. You currently feel frustrated because you are not able to always effectively control the behavior of some students visiting the library in small groups while you are working with entire classes.

CHAPTER 4

Middle School Students

Never humiliate a student in front of others.

Educators who work in middle school settings often comment on the vast differences in physical, emotional, and social development of the students. Frequently, there are dramatic changes in the physical development of middle school students, and some of the students may experience difficulties in coping with the changes. While rapid growth can cause fatigue in some students, generally young adolescents are energetic and need much physical activity to help release some of their energy. Probably the most important overall characteristic of middle school students is their need for acceptance by peers. They are highly sensitive to criticism from their peers. Often, they overreact to ridicule or embarrassment, and yet they can be quite thoughtless and cruel in their relationships with one another. Middle school students have a strong need to belong to a group and often enjoy participating in team sports or school clubs. Some young adolescents also challenge authority and test the limits of acceptable behavior. Yet at the same time, they desire guidance and regulation, and need frequent affirmation from adults.

Because of this tendency to challenge authority and seek independence, it is important that school librarians deal with middle school students in a confident and consistent manner. Establishing positive relationships with middle school students is paramount to gaining the respect of students. Not embarrassing students in front of their peers is essential to building good relationships, as is getting to know the interests of young adolescents. Most discipline or behavior correction should be unobtrusive or conducted apart from the group.

Although academics seem less important to middle school students, they are concerned about their ability to keep up academically with others. Because they tend to prefer active learning to passive, it is wise for a school librarian to include lessons that allow students to work with others and to use skills that relate to real life problems. Middle school students are also developing their sense of humor, so using humor while interacting with students in the library can be an asset to classroom management.

SCHEDULING

In the majority of middle schools, flexible scheduling is the preferred method of arranging student and classroom visits to the library. The school librarian generally keeps a sign-up calendar for classes. The calendar is either physically available in the library or is kept online. Teachers are then able to schedule their classes into the library, with the teachers accompanying their classes. Such a calendar usually works well, and teachers are then able to bring their classes to the library at their times of need, even if it means having a full week of consecutive visits for a research project. Sometimes, the librarian must mediate if more than one teacher wishes to sign up on the calendar and the library is not able to accommodate both classes simultaneously.

Because many school libraries now have their online public access catalogs (OPACs) and other electronic materials accessible from classrooms or from the homes of students, conflicts in scheduling for classes may be lessened. In addition to classes physically utilizing the library, individual students or small groups of students are allowed to visit the library in flexible scheduling. Flexible scheduling has many advantages, including opportunities for students and teachers to use the library facilities at their times of need, as well as making it possible for teachers and school librarians to plan and implement lessons in collaboration with one another.

EFFECTIVE COMMUNICATION

Developing positive relationships with students is critical for middle school librarians. Librarians must learn and understand the unique characteristics of middle school students. An approach that focuses on helping students develop positive, socially appropriate behaviors involves taking personal interest in students. A school librarian should learn the names and interests of students and also be aware of how to serve the needs of all students in a school. Using gentle interventions, avoiding punishments, and developing empathy for young adolescents can contribute to building good student–librarian relationships. Middle school students particularly enjoy humor and usually respond better to remarks that incorporate some type of humor, rather than direct requests.

> Mr. Jones, the school librarian at School #22, often incorporates humor into his lessons and conversations with the students visiting the library. He leisurely walks among the students using the library computers for a lesson and realizes that Josh's screen is on *Froggle* (not one of the sites intended to be used for the lesson). "Are you planning on buying something for everyone in the class?" asks Mr. Jones. Josh shyly smiles, but responds by exiting the site. Another student has his feet on the table. "Do you do that much at home?" inquires Mr. Jones. The atmosphere in the library is relaxed, but the librarian's intentional use of humor is usually successful and results in appropriate student behavior.

Because middle school students do not respond well to being corrected in the presence of their peers, it is a good idea to try to use as many unobtrusive classroom management techniques as possible.

> Mrs. Peters, a middle school librarian at Einstein Middle School, often employs *the look* when a student is not behaving appropriately during a library lesson. Sometimes this is accompanied by a frown. Both of these nonverbal communications bring attention to the misbehavior and communicate a silent request to desist. In almost every instance, this technique seems to work. Other times, she moves near students who are being disruptive and remains in close proximity while she continues with the lesson. If a class is too noisy for her to teach the lesson without raising her voice, she invokes silence and waits until all students are ready to listen or to participate in the activity. These nonverbal communications are easy to use, yet can be very powerful.

RULES AND PROCEDURES

Middle school students quickly lose respect for librarians who have unreasonable policies, who do not maintain the same standards for all students, or whose rules stray towards shades of gray, rather than black and white. Thus, it is important that library rules are fair and consistently enforced. Rules and procedures for middle school libraries must be clearly stated and appear in writing in the student handbook, on the library website, and in an observable place in the library. Since some middle school students tend to push the limits of behavior, there should be quick and consistent correction of any rules that are not followed.

The librarian should conduct a library orientation for incoming 6th grade students, at which time both library rules and procedures are explained. Having a handout with procedures written on them for new students entering the school is recommended. Using some graphics on such a handout will make it more appealing to the students.

Some librarians like to include rules that will keep young adolescents engaged in activities while the students are in the library.

> Ms. Sanchez wants students to be productive when they come to the library at Chavez Middle School. Thus, she has a *productive rule* that she puts into place to help maintain order throughout the day. The students are well aware of the productive rule. If students do not arrive at the library with a particular task to complete, she directs them to sit in the reading area, where she provides graphic novels, magazines, and easy-to-read nonfiction books; thus, the students are encouraged to participate in some type of activity, even while they are relaxing. If students complete what they came to the library to do, she requests them to return to their class or sometimes offers them an opportunity to play educational games on one of the library computers. Ms. Sanchez notes that enforcing this productive rule prevents students from wasting time or coming to the library only to socialize.

It is not unusual for a middle school to have a school-wide prevention approach to discipline. There are a number of such programs, including Consistency Management and Cooperative Discipline (CMCD), Child Development Project (CDP), Positive Behavior Support (PBS), and The Responsive Classroom (RC). If such a program is used in a school or if a school has an adopted discipline policy, it is essential that the school librarian receives training along with classroom teachers, and applies the program principles in the library so that there is consistency throughout the school.

BULLYING

While bullying can happen at any grade level, research has shown that it peaks in the middle school grades. Emotional bullying is the most prevalent, while pushing, shoving, and tripping follow in frequency.

Figure 4.1
Library Orientation Handout for Middle School Students

Edison Middle School Library

FREQUENTLY ASKED QUESTIONS

When is the library open? 7:30 am to 4:00 pm, Monday–Friday

Do I need a library pass? If you come to the library during a school period, you need a pass signed by your teacher. You do not need a pass to visit before school or during your lunch period.

How do I check out a book? Bring the book to the circulation desk and present your school ID card. Books are checked out for four weeks. Only three books may be checked out at a time.

How do I return books? Place them in the brown box on the circulation desk. Speak with a librarian if your books are overdue.

How will I know if a book is overdue? Overdue notices will be delivered to you through your English teacher.

What happens if I lose a book? You will be charged for lost or damaged books.

Can I eat in the library? No candy, drinks, or food are allowed in the library.

Can I use the restroom in the library? Restrooms in the library are for faculty only. Student restrooms are available in the hall.

Can I make copies? You can use the library copy machine ($.10 per page.)

Can I talk and socialize with other students in the library? Be prepared to read or study when you come into the library. If you are disruptive or too loud, you will be asked to leave.

What should I do if I can't find the books or information I need? Ask a librarian if you need help locating materials, or have any other questions.

Cyber bullying (online bullying) is becoming increasingly more common among middle school and high school students and can be even more harmful to the victims because they have no way to escape the bullying.

Often, students are bullied because of sexual orientations, disabilities, religious beliefs, how they look, or ethnic backgrounds (*Bullying*

Statistics). Bullying has long-lasting consequences and is the number one nonacademic issue faced by educators (Bullying.org). Although bullying is more common among boys, it crosses both genders, and the secretive torments that girls participate in by spreading rumors and socially isolating other girls is also considered bullying.

The teachers in a school are one of the keys to bullying prevention. Helping students develop friendships, supervising students at all times, and teaching students to have empathy for others are all important in bullying prevention in a middle school. School librarians can assist in the prevention of bullying by actively dealing with all instances of bullying and being willing to help supervise students in hallways, restrooms, and other areas of the school. Books that deal with bullying should be included in middle school library collections and should be featured in displays, book talks, and book discussions.

Students who are being bullied at school often seek refuge in places that they consider safe, such as a school library. Thus, school librarians must be particularly aware of these students and make certain that their school libraries are indeed safe havens for all students. Librarians should teach students how to recognize bullying and encourage students to report bullying to a responsible adult. A school librarian should also report all bullying to an administrator. Documenting such instances (time, place, and what happened) is essential. All bullying, without exception, should be taken seriously.

CLASS ACTIVITIES

A successful technique in dealing with middle school classes visiting the school library is to have a quiet signal. Middle school students are particularly social, so there are many times that a school librarian must get the attention of students. This can be done with the 5, 4, 3, 2, 1 countdown, the ringing of a bell, or a peace sign. In one school where a large number of students are all using the library simultaneously, the librarian announces in a quiet voice, "If you can hear my voice, clap once." Students who hear, clap once. She then says, "If you hear my voice, clap twice." All students then hear the clapping and know that they are to quiet down and respond by clapping. No matter which quiet signal is used, all students should be trained in the signal that is used in the library. Some patience may be needed; providing middle students a few seconds to complete their all-important conversations is more successful than demanding immediate attention.

Stations (rather than the term *learning centers* used in elementary grades) can be employed successfully in library activities with classes of middle school students:

Mrs. Chan, the school librarian at Williams Middle School, uses stations in her library to teach students how to properly cite material sources. At each station, examples of proper citations are provided for each particular type of format. Students have 15 minutes to complete their source cards at each station by looking through periodicals, searching on computers, and paging through books on a subject of their choosing. After the students complete their source cards and submit them to the librarian or classroom teacher, the students are given a Get Out of Class pass (similar to Monopoly's Get Out of Jail), and they are allowed to visit quietly with other classmates who have completed their source cards. Meanwhile, the librarian and teacher check the cards of students to see if sources are accurately cited. If not, students return to the stations until all cards have accurate citations. The cards are then used in the actual writing of their research papers.

At another middle school, the librarian goes over the criteria for a special project with the class. The students then move to the computers or tables to work on their research projects. The technique of allowing students to work in partnership with one or two other students if desired provides opportunities for students to be a part of a group and have some interaction. If students do not work well together, they are then separated and must complete the project on their own. Most students appreciate the opportunity to work with classmates and stay on task throughout the completion of their projects.

One middle school librarian uses the technique of not repeating herself when teaching a lesson to a class. Because the students are aware of this, they listen carefully, there are few interruptions, and valuable time is not wasted.

Moving among students when they are working on activities in the library is an effective way to manage students and keep them on task. Also, while giving book talks to a classroom of students, the librarian should move to different locations, rather than staying in one spot. This will help engage the attention of young adolescents.

DEALING WITH PROBLEM STUDENTS

Middle school librarians should have immediate, meaningful consequences to implement with difficult students. Dealing with problem students in a middle school library is best done away from the students' peers. The challenging middle school student can often be very adept at manipulating. Thus, it is important not to bargain with such a student. Rather, it is better to focus on the action of the student and not on the student himself. If student behavior is inappropriate and a consequence is employed, then it may be helpful to tell students that you like them and you look forward to their making better choices in the future (Boynton and Boynton 126–28).

Avoiding power struggles is a necessity. Engaging in such struggles can make a school librarian look both foolish and out of control. It is best to concentrate on a long-term positive victory than short-term winning. Such a victory involves changing a potentially negative situation into an opportunity for positive communication. It may be necessary to let other students know that the librarian will be dealing with a difficult student at a later time and redirect attention back to the lesson. It is also important not to carry hostile or angry feelings after a discipline situation has ended (Curwin and Mendler 116–17).

Problem students can easily become emotional in middle school. It is good to have a plan in place for such a situation. If help is needed, then a library clerk or other students can assist by contacting the office via phone or going to a nearby classroom. Another possibility is having a fellow teacher to whom one can send the student for a brief time-out period. Although it might be tempting to try to restrain difficult students during their emotional outbursts, it is best not to intervene physically unless the student is in danger of hurting herself or someone else. Even in such cases, it is wise to call for back-up assistance.

STUDENT VOLUNTEERS

Middle school students can effectively serve as student volunteers in the school library. Volunteers sometimes come to the library during study hall periods, or in some schools, they take an elective course as a library aide and receive grades for their service. In either case, serving as student library aides provides young adolescents with real-world work experience. Students should complete an application form that is similar to a real job application. On such an application they can list references, share why they want to work in the library, and note any experience they have had that might be helpful to them as a library aide. The school librarian can then talk with classroom teachers about which students they would recommend as library aides. It is important not to take too many students into such a program and to select students that have the potential of being good workers (Schipman 26).

Middle school library aides need to be trained to work in the library. They should be told about the importance of acting professionally, as well as maintaining the privacy of students (not sharing or commenting on what materials students check out of the library). The library aides can perform a variety of tasks including shelving books, checking in and out materials, creating bulletin boards and displays, gathering materials for class projects, and even making PowerPoint presentations or videos to be used in the school library orientation.

WORKING WITH TEACHERS AND SUPPORT STAFF

Because many middle school libraries are flexibly scheduled, the librarians have numerous opportunities to collaborate with other teachers. Middle schools are generally set up with teams of teachers who are responsible for the same group of students. A school librarian should plan on attending as many of the teacher team meetings as possible. In this way, the librarian can become aware of the curriculum being taught by each team and can actively participate in planning.

Middle schools are often places where rich collaborative partnerships can take place. Since middle school teachers are used to the idea of working with other educators to meet the needs of their students, they usually welcome the school librarian into planning collaborative lessons. Collaborative lesson plans should be used whenever the school librarian has an opportunity to plan and implement a lesson with one or more teachers. With realistic goals and expectations for the students, engaging lesson plans can be made for every class.

A middle school library that uses flexible scheduling may have one or more classes using the library simultaneously. The demands for services of the school librarian may be great. In one middle school library, the librarian has a Now Serving Board that works quite the same way as a busy deli where customers take a number and wait for service. On the library's Now Serving Board there are two hooks. On one hook there are 20 number cards starting with number 1. If students need the assistance of the school librarian, they take the next available number and continue working on their class project while waiting for the number to be called. The librarian notes that the boards are easy and inexpensive to make.

At another middle school, the team members and school librarian often plan lessons in which students can get up and move about the library. Sometimes the lessons include scavenger hunts or teams answering questions, with members of the team walking quickly up to the circulation desk to ring a bell when they have correct answers.

Figure 4.2
Collaborative Lesson Plan

Collaborative Lesson Plan

Collaborators _____

Grade Level _____

Time Frame _____

Project Goal _____

Specific Objectives _____

Curriculum Standards Addressed _____

Information Literacy Standards Addressed _____

_____

Resources Needed _____

_____

Librarian Responsibilities	Teacher Responsibilities
_____	_____
_____	_____
_____	_____
_____	_____

Project Assessment _____

_____

_____

_____

Riverside
Middle School
Library

Since the library is a large open area, such activities make it possible for the energetic middle school students to move physically and be in a more relaxed atmosphere than found in the typical classroom.

Many of the research projects in which middle school students participate require the use of both print and electronic sources. School librarians can plan with teachers on how those resources will be utilized in the library.

Ms. Gold often plans lessons with teachers at Harding Middle School. When a social studies teacher and Ms. Gold collaboratively planned a lesson in which the students were to focus on various Native American Indian tribes, Ms. Gold gathered all the books in the library collection on the subject of Native Americans. She then placed them on the library tables according to the tribes and the part of the country in which the tribes were located. When the students arrived in the library, they sat at the tables that corresponded to the tribes they had been assigned. Ms. Gold gave a brief presentation on Native Americans and discussed the assignment and available materials in the library. The students were then divided up alphabetically according to their last names, and half of the students were told to work on the project using the print materials, while the other half used the computers to search on the Internet. The following day, the students switched research methods. During both days, the school librarian and teacher walked around and helped students locate the information they needed for their assignment. At the end of each class period the students were asked to leave their print materials on the tables where they were found so students in the next social studies class coming to the library would be able to use the materials. This simple method used by Ms. Gold insured that every class that was working on the project in the library had the same chance to use print and electronic materials.

In a middle school library that uses flexible scheduling, it is particularly helpful to have full-time support staff. It is generally more difficult to obtain parent volunteers in secondary school settings, and yet the need is great for assistance in the middle school library. Support staff adults need to both like and understand middle school students. These are probably the most important requirements for a position in a middle school library. Even though parents of middle school students might apply for such a position, it may not always be wise to have parents working in the same school as their children. This can sometimes create problems with students' peers; each situation, however, may be different.

SUMMARY

Since most middle schools use flexible scheduling for their libraries, teachers and librarians have many opportunities to plan lessons collaboratively. Students are also able to use library facilities and materials as often as needed. All personnel working in a school library should understand the unique characteristics of middle school students and show sincere interest in the students. Written rules and procedures should be clearly stated and applied with consistency in order to gain and maintain the respect of students. Discipline is most effective if implemented away from peers. Middle school students enjoy humor and being with their peers; thus, lessons that incorporate some humor and provide for group work often work well. Bullying is a huge concern in middle schools today. All educators in a school need to work together to implement effective bullying prevention programs and to be diligent in supervising students. Every case of bullying should be taken seriously and dealt with immediately.

SCENARIOS

Think about or discuss how you could handle the following situations:

1. You are a school librarian in a middle school and have a part-time clerk who works in the library for three periods during the day, including the period that you take a half-hour lunch break. Each day when you return from lunch in the cafeteria, the clerk reports that she has had many discipline problems with students, and you feel guilty about taking time away from the library for lunch.
2. When one social studies class comes to the middle school library where you are the librarian, there are a few students who are disruptive, and they seem to set the tone for the entire class. How can you change the personality of the group?
3. Valerie is an attractive 7th grade library volunteer. When boys come to the library, they tend to hang out at the circulation desk and talk to Valerie for long periods of time.

CHAPTER 5

High School Students

Be a teacher—not a friend.

Although it may seem like some high school students are adults, it is important to remember that they are still developing as individuals, do not always make good judgments, and need guidance. Teachers, including school librarians, should not be friends or buddies with students. A school librarian should be professional with all students and demonstrate clearly by words and actions that the librarian cares about students but is in charge. Treating students with kindness, courtesy, and sincere interest can be accomplished while still remaining an authority figure.

Vast differences exist between ninth- and twelfth-grade students, yet a few general characteristics of high school students can be noted. Teenagers are experimenting with adult-like relationships. They enjoy co-educational activities, and are both internally and externally motivated. In their learning, they are capable of abstract thinking. Adolescents need to understand the purpose and relevance of instructional activities. Most high school students want adults to assume a support role in their education. The teens themselves want to assume individual responsibility for their learning, and they want to establish personal long-term goals. Teens also need support and opportunities for self-expression (Pennington).

SCHEDULING

Almost all high schools use flexible scheduling for their libraries. In addition to one or more teachers being able to schedule their classes into the library by means of a library calendar, individual and small groups of students are allowed to visit the library for a variety of purposes. Often, these students come from study halls. In some schools, these students are required to have specific tasks that they are to work on while in the library, but in other schools students may simply visit the library because they have spare time.

High school librarians handle individual visits made by students to the library in a variety of ways. Unlike many elementary schools, high school students are usually not allowed to leave class and be in the halls without a pass, so in most high schools, a pass of some type is required to visit the library. The librarian accepts the pass, makes certain the time leaving the class has been recorded, and that a teacher has signed the pass. Some librarians document the student's name and the time entering in the library on an additional form. If students remain in the library for an entire period, the librarian might return the passes to classroom teachers by placing them in the appropriate teacher mailboxes at the end of the day. On the other hand, if a student returns to the classroom, the librarian signs the pass and records on the pass the time the student left the library. In some schools, students simply sign in and out on a form kept near the library entrance.

It is a good idea for school librarians to have a policy relating to the use of the library by study hall students or students coming from classes to use the library facilities. Introducing a draft of such a policy at a faculty meeting and receiving input about it from classroom teachers and administrators will help all school personnel take ownership of the policy and be willing to help enforce the procedures. Figure 5.1 is a sample of such a policy.

Flexible scheduling in high schools also makes it possible for librarians to plan and implement lessons with classroom teachers. Generally, librarians are most successful in such collaborative activities when working with English and social studies teachers, since those courses are the ones that tend to include research projects in their curricula. However, school librarians should encourage collaboration with all classroom teachers.

Some high school librarians strive to have their libraries open both before and after the school day in order to provide opportunities for all students to have access to the library materials or because school

Figure 5.1
Student Use of the School Library

Nottingham
High School
L I B R A R Y

Student Use Guidelines

- Students may come to the library without a pass in the morning before classes and in the afternoon after dismissal.

- During school hours, students must have a library-related purpose to visit the library. Homework assignments should be completed in study hall unless they require use of library materials.

- Use the **color-coded passes** available from your teachers.

    - **BLUE** (Long Pass): for students needing to use the library materials for the entire class period. You must remain in the library until the bell rings. Only 4 or less students per classroom may come to the library using this pass.

    - **YELLOW** (Short Pass): for students needing to use the library (perhaps to check out or return materials) for up to 15 minutes. A librarian must sign your pass when you leave. Return directly to study hall or your class. Only 3 or less students at a time per classroom may use this pass.

- Students with passes must come directly to the library from their classroom or study hall. Sign in and leave your passes with the librarian or clerk at the circulation desk.

- Students with passes must sit in designated areas of the library and are not to sit with or disturb students who are in the library with a class.

- Students are expected to work quietly and will be sent back to classrooms for inappropriate behavior. Students who are asked to leave may not return to the library for one week.

- Students in scheduled classes have priority use of the computers.

administrators request extended hours. This may create scheduling problems for librarians, particularly if the librarians are expected to have longer work hours than classroom teachers.

A large number of buses transport students to Oakwood High School. The students begin arriving 45 minutes before classes begin. To maintain order in the school, the administrators made the decision to have all students either report to the gymnasium when they arrive at school or go to the library. No students are to be in the halls unless attending prearranged visits to classrooms to meet with teachers. The physical education teachers are expected to supervise the students in the gymnasium, while Ms. Winter, the school librarian, has the assignment of overseeing students in the library. On many days there are more than 100 students in the library before the bell rings for the first class to begin. The library is also open for an hour after school, but many fewer students use the library facilities during that time. Ms. Winter met with her library clerk and asked if the clerk would be willing to come in to work a half hour early in the morning and perform the routines of opening up the library, booting up computers, and supervising the first few students arriving at school in exchange for leaving work a half hour early at the end of the day. Ms. Winter then arrives at work when more students are present in the library in the mornings; after school, when fewer students are utilizing the library facilities, she works alone. This staggered scheduling of the clerk and Ms. Winter's work hours, although not ideal, seems to be the best solution that they currently can manage.

Before school, the library personnel reserve one section of the library for students who want to study or work on school projects. However, because many of the students do not have academic needs, other students are allowed to quietly socialize, as long as they do not disturb students beyond their tables. The library also subscribes to several popular teen magazines and some newspapers that are available to the students; they are in high demand during this time before classes, as are the numerous graphic novels in the library collection.

During the day, it is also possible for a large number of students to be present simultaneously in a high school library, including multiple classes plus individual students. Therefore, it is important that high school librarians have excellent organizational and student management skills in order to maintain an effective learning environment.

EFFECTIVE COMMUNICATION

Expectation of good conduct and respect for students are two important school librarian characteristics that promote effective classroom management in a high school library. Librarians who genuinely care about students, listen to them, know the students, are aware of what classes they are in, and express interest in things that teenagers care about tend to get respect from students. By attending extracurricular activities such as sports competitions, concerts, and school plays, high school librarians demonstrate their interest in students. Librarians who do not have a special interest in adolescents or in school activities will most likely have more difficulty communicating with high school students.

Although high school students appreciate humor and might respond well to it when used for classroom management, sarcasm should never be used. Humor that is used at the expense of a student's dignity is unprofessional and cruel (Boynton and Boynton 92).

School librarians must also be careful of how praise is employed with high school students. Compliments given to adolescents in front of their peers have the potential of being embarrassing and unwanted. It is often better to commend or compliment high school students in private settings. Praise must always be age appropriate.

However, like all students, a friendly greeting from the librarian is appreciated and sets a welcoming atmosphere in a high school library. Although it might be difficult to know all the students' names in a high school, using their names when addressing them is an effective management strategy. Keeping a copy of the school yearbook in the librarian's office and referring to it helps a librarian put names with faces, as does looking for defining characteristics of students and relating them to students' names.

> Each student that enters the City Honors High School Library is welcomed with a smile by Ms. Clark, the school librarian. She never barks at students, demeans them, or talks down to them. She treats all students, whether she truly likes them or not, with kindness and respect. In turn, they treat her the same way. This makes it easier for her to operate the library effectively and to conduct classes with ease since she does not have to reprimand students or work hard to gain their attention. She shows by example how mature people treat one another and subsequently is treated well by the students.

RULES AND PROCEDURES

High school librarians who communicate fair and reasonable policies at the beginning of a school year and expect, rather than demand, that students abide by them from day one seem to have far more success than those who fail in these aspects. The expectation of good conduct, as opposed to the demand for it, is one of the factors that students see as an indicator of a librarian's respect for them as people.

A cardinal rule for students in a library should be some form of the Golden Rule: Do to others what you wish them to do to you. Having respect for others means a reduction in misbehaviors and possible conflicts.

Another suggestion for a library rule in a high school is to tell students the acceptable number of students who are allowed to sit at a table. Since high school students are very social, it is not unusual for them to move chairs or even tables to accommodate a large number of students. They should be instructed not to rearrange furniture unless asked by the librarian to do so. Asking them to remain in their seats until the bell rings and to push chairs back up to the table will help maintain orderly exits from the library, as well as save a librarian's time in straightening the library before other students arrive.

Food and drink may also be problematic in a high school library. Except for special events, it is generally best not to allow open food and drink in a library, because of the damage it can do to materials, computers, or furniture. Such a rule must apply equally to faculty members, even when they bring in their cups of coffee to read the morning newspaper during their planning periods. Providing a separate room out of student view for teachers to relax for such an activity may be a viable alternative.

Gum and tobacco chewing can also create problems in a library, especially if the gum and tobacco are not disposed of properly. It is best not to have either of these items used in a library, but if gum chewing is not banned throughout the school, enforcing a no-gum-chewing policy in the library is extremely difficult and time consuming. It is then more effective to remind students about the proper disposal of chewed gum. Setting reasonable rules involves thought and sometimes experimentation. Not all rules can be anticipated, and new rules may need to be added when circumstances tend to require them (Gootman 40).

Since all students in most high schools are enrolled in an English course in the ninth grade, it is recommended that school librarians arrange for library visits with each English class early in the school year. Conducting a library orientation for these students helps the students understand library policies and procedures, and introduces students to the many materials that are available both in the library itself and through electronic access. Such an orientation will have more impact if a librarian uses an interesting video in which students from the school appear or provides a scavenger hunt that requires using library materials.

Other students sometimes help enforce library rules by reminding students of rules or appropriate behavior.

At Jefferson High School, the school librarian, Mr. Hammer, explains the rules and procedures to incoming freshmen at special library orientations arranged through their English teachers. However, he reports that it generally takes a semester before some of the ninth-grade students behave appropriately in the library. When he became a new school librarian a few years ago, he said that he accidentally found a way that helped speed along this process. When a small group of ninth-grade boys became very noisy, some seniors who were using the library got on them by saying things such as, "Hey, you kids, stop acting like sixth graders." Immediately, the boys stopped their loud talking and laughing. Now when younger students misbehave in the beginning weeks of the academic year, Mr. Hammer waits a few moments to see if older students will make remarks to the students or give them looks of disapproval. He reports that when they do so, it seems to be much more successful in changing the disruptive behavior than when Mr. Hammer corrects the students. "I do talk to students about their misbehavior when necessary, but I find this small amount of peer pressure from older students can serve as a very effective deterrent," states Mr. Hammer.

If it becomes necessary to take away library privileges from a student, it is best that a brief period of time initially be invoked. For instance, for a first offense, students may receive a warning. For a second offense, a week without library privileges may be the consequence. Only for continuous offenses should a student lose library privileges for an entire semester. If a student is required to be in the library for a project and is accompanied by a classroom teacher, the teacher should be informed of the student's discipline problem. If the teacher is not able to supervise students so that they are behaving appropriately, then a disciplinary referral to a school administrator may be needed.

It is usually best for a librarian to try to handle student misbehavior, if possible. However, if behavior violates school policy, such as swearing at other students or a threatening a teacher, then the librarian should immediately send the student to a school administrator. More flexibility in consequences can be used when students are not complying with library rules. In any case, consequences for inappropriate behavior should be logical and clearly linked to a student's behavior.

Requesting students to repeatedly write, "I will behave in the library" is not a relevant consequence for high school students. However, asking a student to come into the library and remove gum from the bottom of tables may be appropriate if a librarian sees a high school student stick a wad of chewing gum in a book or under a library table.

Since it is very difficult for a school librarian to remember the consequences that he invokes for student misbehavior in a large high school, it is wise to document any major library rules that are broken. The discipline record form used in Figure 5.2 can assist in such documentation.

When using a discipline record, it is important for a librarian to ask a high school student to accompany the librarian to a setting that is away from student peers (perhaps to the librarian's office or the circulation desk). The librarian then must determine the student's name. High school students sometimes do not report their correct names, so it may be necessary to ask a student for photo identification. Most high schools distribute such cards to students. Often, just writing the names of students on the discipline record will make students aware of the fact that inappropriate behaviors are being recorded. A warning at that time might be sufficient to alter future behavior problems with a particular student.

Keeping a discipline record can be extremely beneficial if a school librarian has continuous problems with a student and needs to refer the student to a school administrator. School librarians who consistently use a discipline record find that the number of behavior instances that need to be documented in a semester goes down rapidly as word of the strategy spreads among the students.

BULLYING

Bullying is a growing problem in all secondary schools. For this reason, it must be directly addressed in schools. Bullying entails repeated, intentional harm, either physical or emotional. Cyberspace is a more recent venue for bullying and has potential of inflicting serious harm. It has been reported that much of the bullying in high schools happens when students are unsupervised in hallways or restrooms. For this reason, many schools ask teachers to help supervise students in the halls between classes and sometimes assign restroom supervision duties to teachers, paraprofessionals, or even administrators.

Because bullying can constitute violence under the No Child Left Behind Act (NCLB), schools must also confront the issue or be at risk of

Figure 5.2
Discipline Record

DISCIPLINE RECORD SHEET

Student Name	Date	Rule(s) Broken	Consequences Provided

being labeled an unsafe school. However, even without this pressure, it is imperative that schools work to eliminate bullying (Gootman 160).

Many high schools have developed anti-bullying policies that emphasize prevention and student reporting of bullying instances. A school librarian should be aware of such policies and be constantly on the lookout for bullying in the library and hallways. No instance of bullying should go unreported, and all instances should be documented. It is especially important that students who are frequently the victims of bullies are able to feel safe in school libraries. Victims often include gay students, teens from diverse ethnic backgrounds, and students who just seem different and may have difficulty fitting in socially. Jealousy, particularly on the part of girls, also frequently contributes to bullying.

CLASS ACTIVITIES

In high schools, librarians are able to easily plan and work with classroom teachers. Typical all-class activities include teaching the research process, helping students create science projects, providing opportunities for students to respond to the books they have read, or teaching information literacy skills. When teachers successfully plan lessons with the librarian, the word often spreads and other teachers are more apt to be willing to collaborate. Reporting on a successful collaborative project at a faculty meeting or in a school newsletter will also provide an opportunity for other teachers to see how a librarian can assist teachers with their curriculum goals and objectives.

If misbehavior occurs when students from a class are working in the library, it may be necessary to communicate with the classroom teacher who is in charge of supervising the students. Sometimes simply approaching talkative students to ask them if they need some assistance will help get them back on task. A librarian may also choose to remind students what is expected of them. Nonverbal messages also work well with many high school students.

At Valley High, Mrs. Chan uses both humor and nonverbal communication to correct behavior. Recently when a student visiting the library with a class was sitting on top of one of the book stacks, Mrs. Chan quietly called his name to gain his attention, and then used humorous hand gestures and charades to ask him to get off the stacks. Finally, she smiled. Mrs. Chan explained that she tries to always end a behavior request with a smile. In this way, students know that what they did was wrong, but it was the behavior that was not wanted, not the student.

In all cases when a high school teacher brings an entire class to the library, the classroom teacher should accompany the class. The library should not be employed as a dumping ground for a teacher who wants to have an hour off. Unfortunately, there are some teachers who do not always follow library or school policy in this regard:

Mr. Paulis, a science teacher at Southwest High School, frequently takes his class to the library. In most instances, he provides little or no notice of his class visits to the library, nor does he plan lessons with the librarian. During the past few times that he sent a class to the library, he did not show up until at least 15 minutes after the students arrived. By e-mail, Ms. Henry, the school librarian, reminded him of the library policy that teachers need to accompany their students to the library, but he responded that he needed time to gather his materials or talk to a few students in the class. Ms. Henry also explained in her e-mail that sometimes she has not been informed of the students' assignment and thus is not prepared to assist them. The next day when Mr. Paulis did not appear in the 15 minutes after one of his classes arrived, Ms. Henry decided to call the school office, explain the situation, and see if he could be located. After the vice-principal personally went in search of Mr. Paulis, his tardiness in the library no longer occurred.

Although it is unfortunate that school librarians must occasionally apply pressure for teacher compliance with library policies, it is necessary that policies apply to all teachers equally, just as rules should be employed consistently with all students. There may be emergency times when a librarian needs to step in and help manage a class, but favoritism should never be a regular part of dealing with faculty members.

DEALING WITH PROBLEM STUDENTS

Problem students in a high school are particularly adept at trying to draw teachers or librarians into power struggles. Such conflicts involve participants attempting to control the attitudes and actions of others by using threats or defiance. It is important to recognize when a student is attempting to draw an authority figure into a power struggle and then to respond by not taking the bait. Admittedly, this is not always easy. However, one of the first responses that a school librarian can make in such a situation is to try to disengage one's emotions. This might involve taking some deep breaths, counting to 10 before responding, or simply walking away for a short personal time-out. The librarian should then respond to the student, in a private location if at all possible. Speaking in a quiet, calm voice, using the student's name, and being willing to listen to the student will help de-escalate the situation before following through with consequences for inappropriate behavior. Invoking consequences when one is angry or upset can sometimes lead to regrettable actions on the part of a school librarian. A librarian should not allow a student to be an attorney and argue about a consequence. If the misbehavior and consequence have been clearly communicated, then the time for argument should be over (Boynton and Boynton 115). Later, if librarians feel as if the consequence was perhaps not totally justified, they should not hesitate to make any needed apologies or to alter the consequences.

Physical student fighting tends to be more prevalent in secondary schools than in elementary schools. It is wise for a school librarian not to get involved in student fights in a high school setting, but instead call for assistance as quickly as possible. Many high school students are physically very strong and can inflict serious harm on adults who try to intervene. Some high schools have emergency response teams available for needed assistance, and it is also possible that police may need to be called in, depending on the severity of possible harm.

Theft and intentional damage to materials can also be an issue in high school libraries. Having ways for students to inexpensively copy or print out materials or providing for flexible circulation of reference materials can help cut down on theft and damage to materials. The use of security systems is much more prevalent in high school libraries than in other grade levels. Additionally, having good relationships with students will lessen both theft and damage problems.

WORKING WITH TEACHERS AND SUPPORT STAFF

Clearly defined policies and procedures not only help students, but they also provide guidance to teachers and library staff. Since teachers are often present in the library with their classes, they need to be aware of library policies and behavior expectations. Providing the faculty with written copies of these can help make collaborative lesson implementation flow much more smoothly. It should be the goal of all authority figures in the library to create a climate where students can engage in appropriate behavior. Library clerks must be carefully trained in enforcing rules and procedures; any problems in this area should be discussed in private and not in front of students. Two or more school librarians sharing duties in a high school library must also be in agreement on rules and their enforcement. Inconsistent enforcement of procedures or policies can be extremely confusing to students and can cause relationship problems between authority figures.

Student volunteers can be very helpful in high school libraries. Often, these volunteers are students coming from study halls or perhaps are students who do not eat lunch, but spend their lunch period in the library. Again, these volunteers must be carefully trained and should follow all procedures consistently. They should not be expected to handle discipline problems, but should be encouraged to report any possible problems to the librarian. Often, student volunteers are used to man the circulation desk and to possibly gather and document student passes. If they are not working on class assignments, the student volunteers might offer to help with other library duties, but most often if students come from study halls, they have a need to complete their own school work.

If a school has a work study program, it is a good idea to offer student placement in the library. In such cases, the students in the program are receiving either credit or actual salaries for their work. These students should be trained in a variety of library tasks including checking in and out materials, shelving books, repairing materials, helping students locate materials, processing books, creating bulletin boards and displays, assisting in collection development, and even in helping other students who are having difficulty with online searching. It is not unusual for students who work in libraries to later select librarianship as a career or to apply to work as paraprofessionals in school or public libraries. Therefore, it is important to treat these students well and to provide to them as many opportunities as possible.

SUMMARY

Since almost all high school libraries use a flexible schedule, librarians working in such settings need to have the personality and skills to work well with teenage students, as well as with teachers and other personnel who are employed in the library. Reasonable student rules and procedures that emphasize respect for adolescents must be consistently enforced. Consequences for inappropriate behaviors should be clearly communicated and linked logically to misbehaviors. Problems and issues in high school libraries often differ from other grade levels and have the potential of being more serious. Bullying is currently a prevalent problem throughout high schools; thus, school librarians must watch carefully for any cases of bullying and make certain that their libraries are safe environments for all students.

SCENARIOS

Think about or discuss how you could handle the following situations:

1. You are a high school librarian in a large school that has two professional school librarians. The other librarian has rules that are much more liberal than yours, and you always seem to come out looking rigid and strict to the students. When you discipline students for disruptive behavior, you hear, "Mr. Miller lets us do that. Why can't you?"

2. You are a school librarian in a high school that opens a half hour before classes begin in the morning. A group of four students come to the library every morning. They sit together at a table and are very noisy, bothering students at nearby tables. You have talked to the four students several times, but have seen no improvement in their behavior.

3. Kate is a very attractive, socially oriented student who comes into your high school library each noon hour. She talks almost continually, and you have asked her to quiet down several times. Yesterday, you took her into your office and discussed the problem with her. Together you made a plan to have her sit alone at a small table for a two-week trial period. One of the high school coaches came to the library today. He sat down with Kate, began talking to her, and openly flirted with her.

CHAPTER 6

Students from Diverse Backgrounds

Know your students' interests, backgrounds, and needs.

The student population in U.S. schools is becoming increasingly diverse. This includes not only students from different religious, race, and ethnic backgrounds, but also students with special needs, such as those with disabilities. For instance, in 1984, approximately one in four school children were minority students, but by 2020 it is predicted that figure will likely increase to one in two (Shaw). With a recent wave of immigration to the United States, the enrollment of Hispanic and Asian students has increased by more than 5 million since the 1990s (*New York Times*). An estimated five million English language learners (ELLs) currently live in the United States, with Hispanic students comprising 75 percent of this student group (Nichols 26).

Many disabilities are also are the rise. Recent studies indicate that three of every 1,000 children between the ages of three and ten suffer from autism, and it is estimated that nearly 4 million children will be diagnosed with autism in the next 10 years (Nichols 20).

Students with special needs are more frequently receiving some or all of their education in general education classrooms, as well as in the school library. Young people with a variety of disabilities are often mainstreamed into classes for part of a day. Additionally, many school districts currently have inclusive classrooms in which all diverse students are included with regular students during the entire day.

Some of the students who may have special needs include those with the following:

- mental disabilities
- learning disabilities
- emotional disabilities
- physical disabilities (visual, hearing, or mobile impairments)
- chronic illnesses
- attention deficit disorders
- at-risk backgrounds
- transient family backgrounds—such as migrants and the homeless

In some instances, there are federal laws that relate to specific groups of students. Currently in the United States, access to equal education for every child is a national policy. However, this has not always been the case. Not until the 14th Constitutional Amendment was adopted in 1868 and legal cases such as *Brown v The Board of Education* were brought before the U.S. Supreme Court in the 1950s and 1960s were there equal educational opportunities for African American students.

The passage of the Education for All Handicapped Children Act in 1975, which was later renamed the Individuals with Disabilities Education Act of 2004 (IDEA), was intended to correct some of the problems that children with special needs were experiencing in U.S. public schools. IDEA requires that to the maximum extent appropriate, students with special needs be educated in the least restrictive environment. It also requires that individualized educational programs (IEPs) be made for such students (Logsdon). In 1991, the Americans with Disabilities Act (ADA) was signed into law; it added many provisions for the needs of persons with disabilities, not only in schools but in other public institutions and places of employment.

The No Child Left Behind Act (NCLB) signed into federal law in 2002 mandates that all students will succeed (defined as being on grade level) by the year 2013. The promise of academic success includes students with disabilities, as well as students whose native language is not English. Thus, these students are tested along with other students, and the schools in which they are enrolled are accountable for their academic success (Hardman and Dawson 5–6). The McKinney-Vento Homeless Assistance Act is the primary piece of federal legislation dealing with the education of children and youth experiencing homelessness in U.S. public schools. It was passed and signed into law by President Ronald Reagan in 1987 and has been amended several times. It was reauthorized as Title X, Part C, of NCLB in 2002 and provides for expanded resources for homeless students. McKinney-Vento ensures that homeless children are transported free of charge to a public school of their choice in their school district. It also ensures immediate enrollment of students in a school, regardless of unpaid fines at previous schools (National Association for Homeless Education at the SERVE Center).

EFFECTIVE COMMUNICATION

Many of the same techniques for communicating with regular students can be used to effectively communicate with students from diverse backgrounds or with students who have special needs. These include caring about students, showing genuine interest in them, treating them with respect, and listening to their concerns. Being aware of some of the characteristics of particular cultures or the special needs of students with disabilities can contribute to positive communication with these students.

The following are a few explanations of some general characteristics of particular groups of students; note that these characteristics do not necessarily relate to all young people in the groups. Keeping these characteristics in mind can help librarians effectively communicate with students from particular ethnic backgrounds or young people with special needs.

- Some Native American children have a rich culture in nonverbal language and may express themselves through body language, rather than words. They may speak softly and slowly, and they avoid eye contact, which is considered unacceptable in communicating with elders.
- Family honor is extremely important to Chinese American young people. Thus, they may suppress any personal problems and not be willing to discuss them.
- Among first generation Japanese American children, very little eye contact is made. Eye contact is considered impolite, particularly when communicating with older persons.
- Vietnamese American young people consider it rude to look someone straight in the eye or to disagree with them openly. They may smile and say "yes," even when they are upset, so they do not hurt others' feelings.
- Mexican Americans are likely to be sensitive to the feelings and opinions of others. They also are more likely than Anglos to want

to touch, taste, feel, or be close to an object or person on which attention is focused.

- Humility is a highly valued expectation among Puerto Rican Americans. Children lower their eyes and heads to show respect to elders.
- Autism encompasses a very wide spectrum of behaviors and learning problems. Some children with autism are completely nonverbal, while others, such as those with Asperger's syndrome, can be very talkative.
- Students with autism tend to be visual learners. It is beneficial to have a note pad and pen handy if asking a question or making a request, so a simple picture can be drawn.
- Young people with autism can often be calmed by doing a task, such as carrying some books or passing out materials for a lesson.
- When speaking to autistic students, it is best to use language that is simple and concrete; idioms and jokes should be avoided.
- Many autistic persons have difficulty making eye contact; this should not be considered a lack of respect or inattention.
- Students with autism often do not understand other people's thoughts and motivations and may respond to situations inappropriately. They may not be able to form relationships with other students and should not be forced into group activities in which they are experiencing much discomfort.
- When speaking with students who are beginning to learn English, one should speak slowly and clearly, pausing frequently and simplifying vocabulary when necessary.
- For older ELLs, providing a glossary of terms will help the students learn library terminology and use information resources.
- School librarians should try to learn and use the names of ELL students, even though some names may be very challenging.
- If possible, librarians should provide translated copies of library policies to ELL students and their families.
- Learning some signs to use with students who are hearing impaired will help with communication. One should not shout at these students.
- Librarians should sit down or bend down to talk with students in wheelchairs; in other words, it is important to get on the students' level.
- Librarians should not be afraid to ask young people about their disabilities and how to help them.

RULES AND PROCEDURES

If library rules are reasonable and broad enough, there is usually no reason to alter them for students from diverse backgrounds or for students with special needs. Having a rule such as, "All students will sit quietly with their hands folded in their laps and will listen attentively during story time" is much too specific and not reasonable for some young children with special needs. However, if rules generally address respect for others and for materials in the library, all students can be expected to abide by such rules. Of course, students must understand both rules and procedures. Using pictorial representations or charades to explain procedures is helpful to students whose native language is not English. Modeling and providing practice for library procedures can be very helpful to many students with special needs. Clear statements of positive consequences for following the rules, as well as consequences for violating rules need to be explained to students. Compassion may need to be exercised in the enforcement of rules and procedures; the ultimate goal should be to teach students responsibility.

Inclusion of all students in a library program can provide an excellent way to model how people should treat one another with respect and dignity. It is important for school librarians to recognize that each child has distinctive needs; yet, all students have the same basic needs of being respected and valued.

BULLYING

It is particularly sad that the students who are often suffering from self-esteem problems because of disabilities, race or ethnic background, religion, or sexual orientation are those who are most often the victims of bullying. In the 2007 National School Climate Survey conducted by the Gay, Lesbian, and Straight Education Network (GLSEN), it was found that 86 percent of lesbian, gay, bisexual, or transgender (LGBT) students experienced verbal harassment, 60 percent felt unsafe at school because of their sexual orientation, and 33 percent skipped school because of this (GLSEN). Bullying can take on many shapes and sizes, from mean gossip to physical attack. The bullying behavior itself is unwanted and often relentless.

Many states and school districts require that anti-bullying school programs be in place. Unfortunately, much of the bullying in schools takes place out of the sight of adults, and some bullying is even done in a subtle manner, under an adult's radar. Schools have a particularly hard time fighting online bullying, since most of it occurs in secret or off school grounds. School personnel need to develop anti-bullying programs and create cultures that encourage students to challenge and report instances of bullying. Bullying education should begin in late elementary school, when peer pressure begins to intensify.

School librarians should be proactive in anti-bullying school programs. One of the best ways to do this is to provide resources that deal with bullying. Barnard's (33–39) article in *Young Adult Library Services* lists numerous annotated books and websites on the topic. Librarians can also highlight National Bully Prevention Week, as well as frequently display bullying resources that are available in the library. Additionally, school librarians should always model respectful and tolerant attitudes and, without exception, they should intervene when a student is being bullied. With student cooperation and input, librarians can also help create anti-bullying pledge campaigns.

Although it is more difficult to fight cyber bullying when it takes place outside of school, librarians can be active by educating students about cyber bullying. The topic can be part of cyber safety lessons that are often taught in school libraries. Librarians should tell students to keep records of all bullying messages that are sent to them and not erase them. E-mail and cell phone messages can be traced by the proper authorities, and they can be used as evidence. Students also need to report instances of bullying to a trusted adult: a teacher, parent, guidance counselor, or the police.

CLASS ACTIVITIES

Just as classroom teachers may have to make adjustments in activities for students with special needs, so, too, do school librarians. Without such adjustments, student frustration can negatively affect student learning, and classroom management can become very difficult. For instance, students with attention deficit hyperactivity disorder (ADHD) may not be able to sit for long periods of time.

> Larson Elementary School has an excellent reputation of dealing with special needs children. Parents of such children often request that their children be enrolled in the school. Thus, the school has a student population that is skewed towards special needs students. Ms. Starr, the school librarian, tailors her teaching activities to the needs of the students. With classes that have several students with

attention deficit hyperactivity disorder (ADHD), she incorporates many short activities that often include movement such as dancing, singing, or just some silliness. In the middle of one lesson, she noticed that some of the boys with ADHD clearly needed to get moving. Thus, she momentarily stopped the lesson and asked all students to stand up and move about "to get the wiggles out." She then calmly resumed the lesson, and all students were able to successfully stay on task.

All school librarians and support staff must be aware of the special needs of students. Librarians should read all students' individualized education programs (IEPs). A student's IEP specifies the instructional goals and activities that are appropriate for that particular student with special needs. After reviewing students' IEPs, the librarian can prepare or alter lessons that address the special needs of students. Sometimes, this can mean writing a shorter or clearer version of an assignment for special need students, perhaps asking an autistic student to locate fewer examples in a library orientation scavenger hunt, or producing an assignment worksheet in a larger font for a visually impaired student. Alternate formats, such as videos or digital formats, may need to be used for some students. Assistive technologies can also be used to meet the needs of many students with disabilities. Hopkins notes that "considering its range of resources, you can make a strong case that the library media center is the least restrictive environment of all for many students" (18).

If there are students in a class who do not speak English, this will undoubtedly affect lessons and management of younger children, as described in the following school setting.

Mr. Holmes is a pre-service librarian doing student teaching in South Maple Elementary School. He is very excited, but nervous, about sharing the book and lesson he has prepared for a first-grade class. The school librarian steps out of the library to meet with an administrator and leaves him in charge of the class. After Mr. Holmes begins reading the story, one young boy gets up and starts wandering aimlessly about the library. Mr. Holmes stops his lesson and asks the boy to return to the class, but the boy ignores him and continues walking about. Frustrated that the child is not responding to him, Mr. Holmes again stops his lesson, takes the boy by the hand, and places him in a chair at one of the library tables. There he explains to the boy that he will need to have a time-out for his misbehavior. The child, however, only looks confused and begins to cry.

Finally one of the other children says, "Jose is new in our class. I don't think he understands you."

Because no one had informed Mr. Holmes that Jose did not understand English, this situation was very frustrating to all participants. Had the classroom teacher informed the student teacher that Jose was new and was an ELL, the circumstances could have been altered and not resulted in emotional upsets. Having an aide accompany the class or letting the child quietly wander about to explore the library might have made it possible for the child to have his needs better met and for Mr. Holmes to have successfully taught his class.

When children with special needs are mainstreamed into classes, there are generally some arrangements made for specially trained staff to assist classroom teachers. This is particularly true when students having disabilities require much help or exhibit severely disruptive behaviors. School librarians should request that aides accompany classes with special needs students whenever possible so the librarian is able to effectively deliver lessons, and all students are able to have their needs met. Many schools have special staff development workshops to train their teachers to understand and work with students with special needs. It is important that school librarians be included in such training.

It can be challenging to simultaneously present the same lessons or programs to both students with and without special needs. However, students with disabilities, particularly social deficit disabilities like autism, can learn appropriate behaviors by observing and interacting with other typical students. Facilitating and encouraging group activities in the library also creates opportunities for nondisabled typical students to grow in compassion and not discriminate against individuals who exhibit atypical behaviors. By sharing diverse skills and gifts, young people can gain an understanding and appreciation of differences and learn what it is like to live in a diverse society.

A school library program can make an important contribution to the education of students with disabilities and ELLs by teaching them information skills that will give them lifelong support in accessing information that is important to their daily living. Special education research has demonstrated that students with some special needs, such as those with learning disabilities, respond better to auditory and visual stimuli than to print media (Murray 5). Thus, school librarians can use more multimedia in teaching information skills to such students. As more students with special needs are included in inclusive classes, school librarians need to gather knowledge and information about the most effective ways of managing these students and teaching them information skills. School librarians can learn a great deal about communicating with students with special needs by observing special education teachers and consulting with support professionals such as speech therapists.

DEALING WITH PROBLEM STUDENTS

Students who have been marginalized because of their ethnic backgrounds, sexual orientations, or special needs may be depressed or very frustrated. Emotional pressure put on such students may tend to make them more difficult to manage in classroom settings or in the school library. Thus, some of these students become problem students. It may take several interactions with these students to find the best way to communicate with them or to effectively redirect their energies. A school librarian who has difficulties working with a particular child should not hesitate to ask teachers, parents, or guardians for suggestions. However, students with disorders that put others at risk should be removed from the library and placed in settings where they can receive helpful treatment.

WORKING WITH TEACHERS AND SUPPORT STAFF

The school library is the perfect extension to English as a second language (ESL) programs. Collaborative efforts between ESL teachers and librarians can prove to be fruitful and rewarding. Through collaboration, ESL teachers and librarians can face the challenge of linking students from various cultural backgrounds to information sources. The school librarian should work with ESL teachers to determine which introductory library and information skills should be taught to the various levels of ESL students. These students also need opportunities to use language in meaningful and purposeful interactions with others. School librarians can help provide such opportunities by having students work together in group activities or projects in the library. It is critical that school library collections contain current information about the predominant cultures of a school's population. Librarians can then work with classroom teachers to help provide appropriate resources for ESL students. This will help students gain a feeling of identity and in turn be able to more easily assimilate into the school culture.

School librarians can make unique contributions to meeting students' individualized education programs by serving as instructional consultants to classroom and special education teachers and to support staff who deal with students with special needs. In order to do so, school librarians must be knowledgeable about students' IEPs. After reviewing students' IEPs, librarians can help teachers develop instructional activities and provide expertise in the selection, evaluation, and use of age appropriate materials and emerging technologies. By strengthening the relationships between librarians, teachers, and support staff, the learning barriers for many students can be reduced. This, in turn, will contribute to more effective management of students throughout the school.

All support personnel working with students in a school library need to be aware of the special needs of students in a school. They, like school librarians, should be knowledgeable about the cultural characteristics of students, and they must also be on constant lookout for any occurrences of student bullying.

SUMMARY

To be effective working with students from diverse backgrounds, good communication and collaboration must build between school librarians, classroom teachers, and special education teachers. Good communication and collaboration allows everyone to serve the needs of students from diverse backgrounds and those with special needs. It is a good idea for librarians and support staff to be aware of unique cultural and ethnic characteristics of students. Additionally, they should be trained to meet the needs of special education students who visit the library. When creating rules and managing students in a school library, it is important to remember that although each student may have distinctive needs, all young people have the same basic needs of being respected and valued.

SCENARIOS

Think about or discuss how you could handle the following situations:

1. Steven is a Down syndrome student in middle school who is being mainstreamed for the first time. He desperately wants friends, but is sometimes quite noisy when he comes to the library. A group of boys always make fun of him.

2. You are a school librarian in a high school that serves numerous students whose first language is not English. Many of these students congregate in the library before classes in the morning and sit with other students who have similar ethnic backgrounds. Recently, some students have been getting into loud arguments with students at another table. They are usually not speaking English and so you are not able to understand the conversations or difficulties.

3. Justin is a middle school student with Asperger's syndrome (a high functioning condition on the autism spectrum) who works as a volunteer in your library during his study hall period. He is a good worker and seems to enjoy being in the library, but when students talk to him, he becomes very shy, does not make eye contact with the students, and often does not respond to them. Some students then make negative remarks to him.

CHAPTER 7

Technology

Be prepared for class. A few idle seconds can develop into several problem minutes.

While it is always a good idea to be well prepared to teach a class, it is particularly important when using technology in a lesson. Students will quickly begin to talk or take over computers for their own personal use if a school librarian is not prepared to immediately begin a lesson. Unfortunately, technology problems, such as losing Internet access, sometimes occur; thus, it is valuable to always have backup procedures ready to implement. This may mean printing out a lesson, making some backup transparencies, or simply having another format prepared for the lesson objectives. Although this may seem like much extra work, being able to quickly transfer to an alternate lesson format will not only prevent possible student management problems, but will also make it possible for the same or similar student learning outcomes to be accomplished.

SCHEDULING

The use of student computers varies greatly in school library settings. In some libraries, all student computers are placed in the main area of the library, while others have a separate room or computer lab connected to the library. In the latter case, it is extremely difficult for a librarian to supervise students simultaneously in the library and the computer lab. Extra library personnel need to be available to assist in student supervision.

It is also necessary to note the requirements for technology when a class is being scheduled in the library. In most libraries, class use of computers overrides individual student use. However, depending on the needs of the students, this procedure may vary. If more than one class is scheduled into the library at the same time, as is frequently the case in secondary school libraries, then it is essential that the technology needs are noted in the schedule so that there are no conflicts. A significant amount of technology is integrated into today's lessons; therefore, effective scheduling is paramount.

EFFECTIVE COMMUNICATION

When using technology with students, librarians should communicate not only by using the positive techniques already discussed in previous chapters, but additionally they must learn to converse using technology jargon. Unless a school librarian is a recent graduate of a library science program, this will most likely require some professional development or self-education. It is important that librarians be knowledgeable about technology and be able to discuss technology with both teachers and students. It is very likely that students may have more experience with the new technologies than do librarians or teachers; however, students are not always aware of the ethical or most efficient uses of technologies. Thus, librarians must teach lessons that incorporate topics such as effective search techniques, intellectual property, plagiarism, proper citation of sources, and Internet safety.

RULES AND PROCEDURES

Librarians should establish clear rules and procedures relating to student use of technology. This may involve having students sign up at the circulation desk for the use of numbered computers, maintaining time limitations for computer use, or posting rules relating to the printing of documents. Sometimes particular procedures may need to be established because of misuse of computers or possible theft.

At the Polk High School Library there had been problems with theft of computer mice from the computers in the library computer laboratory. Thus, Mrs. Sweeney, the librarian, implemented a procedure that must be followed by students wanting to use the computers when there are no classes scheduled to use the lab. At the circulation desk students are required to sign in on a sheet to use a computer.

Part of signing in includes signing out a mouse for the computer. A mouse box is kept on a shelf behind the circulation desk, and each mouse is assigned a number written on the bottom of the mouse with a permanent marker. As each student signs up to use the computer, the student must write in the number of the corresponding mouse the student is using. When a student leaves the computer lab, the student is responsible for bringing the mouse back to the circulation desk to check it in. The library aide then checks off on the sign-in sheet that the mouse has been returned. If a mouse turns up missing, the library staff can refer to the sign-in sheet in order to determine where to start looking for the mouse. This procedure gives students a greater sense of responsibility for school property. It also enables the library staff to keep track of how many students use the library each period.

Some school librarians use monitoring programs for their computers. Such programs allow the librarian or library clerk to monitor each of the computers in the library and see what a student is viewing or typing. The library staff can send a message directly to a student's monitor if a student is accessing an inappropriate site and a warning can be given. If a student continues to access sites or write inappropriate messages, then computer privileges can be suspended. The use of such a program may seem like an invasion of privacy to some people, so it is important that the school handbook include a policy regarding the use of computers. Such a policy is often referred to as an *acceptable use policy* (AUP). Numerous examples of AUPs used by specific schools or school districts can be found on the Internet. Although policies may differ somewhat in wording and content, most AUPs include statements about the following:

- General introductory comments relating to the purpose of the policy, including the usefulness of Internet and a statement noting that Internet access is a privilege and not a student right
- Responsibilities of student users (such as following appropriate online behavior and reading and signing an Internet policy)
- Expectations of students (for instance, not expecting that files stored on school-based servers are private, but rather that they can be reviewed by teachers and administrators)
- Unacceptable use of the Internet (disrupting school networks; damaging computer stations; violating copyright or intellectual property rights; plagiarism; accessing pornographic or discriminatory materials; sending materials that threaten, annoy, or

harass; using computers for personal communications; sharing passwords; and using another student's account)
- Guidelines for personal safety when using the Internet (such as not revealing personal information to strangers)
- Statement addressing the fact that the AUP is in compliance with local, state, and federal statutes relating to Internet use
- Sanctions or consequences of violating the AUP (loss of the use of Internet access, possible disciplinary action, or legal action if needed)
- Disclaimer (statements that the school is not responsible for the quality or accuracy of information on the Internet, the loss of data on school-based computers, or financial responsibility for students who access Web sites that require payments)

An acceptable use policy should be written in simple language and should be publicly available. All AUPs should include a form that students and parents sign. Figure 7.1 is an example of such a form that can be part of an AUP and can be detached and returned to school.

After Internet use signature forms are returned to the school, librarians need an efficient procedure to monitor students' use of the Internet.

At Harlee Middle School, Ms. Phillips, the school librarian, makes neon-colored index cards for each student who returns a signed Internet use form. The cards are placed in alphabetical order by last name in a box labeled "Internet Cards" that is kept at the circulation desk. When students come to the library to use a computer, they retrieve their own card and place it in a strategically located cardholder slot on top of the computer that they are using. This allows the library staff to know at a glance who is on the Internet with permission. If students retrieve someone else's card or use the Internet inappropriately, then a dated note of the offense and warning or action is written on the back of the index card. Depending on the degree of the offense and the number of warnings, the student's computer privileges are revoked for a certain period of time. Because the school is relatively small and the school library staff members know the majority of students using the library, this proves to be an efficient and organized way of handling the Internet issue and of managing middle school students while using a fairly unobtrusive approach.

In addition to the use of computers, school librarians may also want to address the use of cell phones, MP3 players, televisions, CDs, DVDs,

Figure 7.1
Signature Form for Internet Use

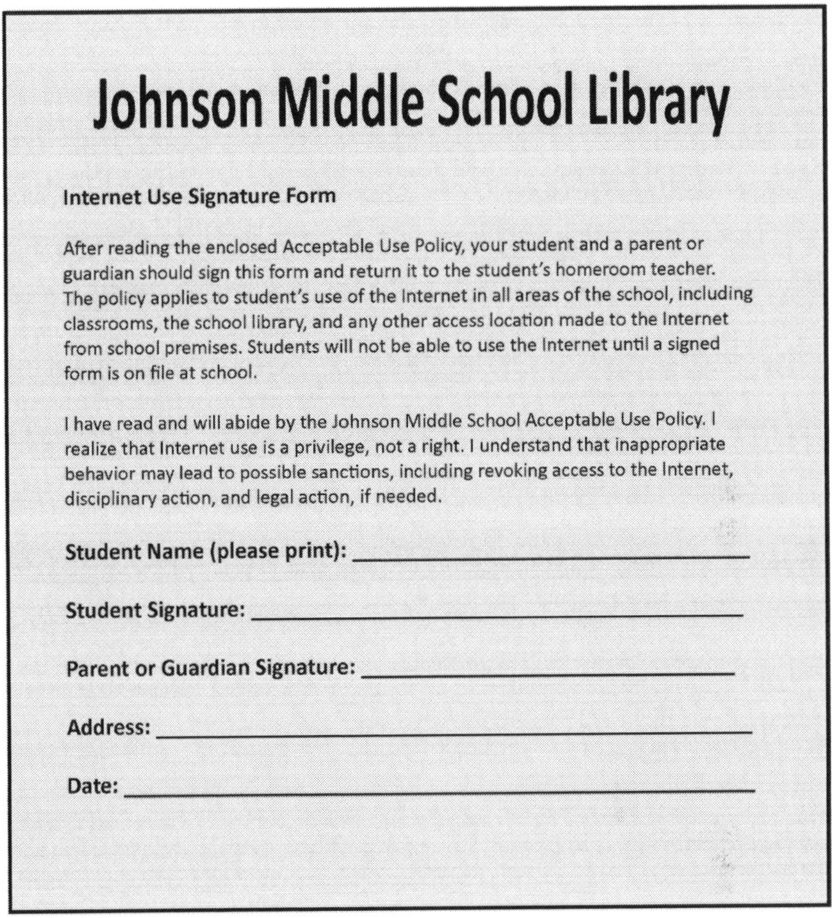

Johnson Middle School Library

Internet Use Signature Form

After reading the enclosed Acceptable Use Policy, your student and a parent or guardian should sign this form and return it to the student's homeroom teacher. The policy applies to student's use of the Internet in all areas of the school, including classrooms, the school library, and any other access location made to the Internet from school premises. Students will not be able to use the Internet until a signed form is on file at school.

I have read and will abide by the Johnson Middle School Acceptable Use Policy. I realize that Internet use is a privilege, not a right. I understand that inappropriate behavior may lead to possible sanctions, including revoking access to the Internet, disciplinary action, and legal action, if needed.

Student Name (please print): _____

Student Signature: _____

Parent or Guardian Signature: _____

Address: _____

Date: _____

printers, cameras, and other technology in the school library. In many schools, there are school-wide policies that deal with all the technologies that might be used in the school. Having such policies makes it possible to more easily educate students and enforce policies fairly throughout the school. School librarians should be certain that they are a part of the school committee that makes these policies.

CLASS ACTIVITIES

Along with writing and enforcing acceptable use policies, school librarians have a responsibility to teach students appropriate and safe

Internet use. These are probably some of the most important lessons that can be taught in secondary school libraries. When teaching lessons, bookmarking the websites that the librarian wants students to access is especially effective in managing students.

The following scenario describes a school librarian who has effectively integrated information technology lessons into a high school setting:

Computer usage is a large part of the students' day at Williams High School. Mr. Douglas, the school librarian, has spent many hours becoming an expert on information and technology in schools. He thus now assumes the major role of informing students about the use of Internet in the school. In well-planned and engaging class lessons, he helps students evaluate the information found online and teaches them critical thinking skills in assessing the veracity of the information. He also teaches lessons that introduce students to the concept of protecting their privacy online, as well as warning of the dangers of sharing personal information. Even though the school receives federal funds and must use Internet blocking software, he tries to offer the students intellectual freedom by using the least restrictive setting of the software and generous use of override lists. As an advocate for the students, Mr. Douglas tries to ensure that all students have access to information technology before, during, and after school hours.

Whenever possible, it is advisable to have computers in a location where library personnel are able to view the screens. When teaching lessons in which all students are using computers at the same time, there are other techniques that can be used to help manage student behavior. For instance, all monitors can be turned off until students are specifically given directions to turn on their monitors. This encourages student attention when the librarian is explaining a lesson, providing directions, or modeling a lesson project. It is helpful if the librarian has a large screen and LCD projector to focus the class's attention on the lesson. All students need to be seated so they are facing the screen. Another helpful tool used in many schools for class lessons is a whiteboard that is connected to a computer so the librarian can easily touch the whiteboard to manipulate information while teaching a lesson.

Some librarians who use a computer lab with a class have students leave every other computer station empty. This tends to cut down on unnecessary chatter and helps students focus on the task at hand.

Many school libraries are now equipped with laptop computers; thus, it is possible to use seating arrangements that fit the needs of the instructor and students. For instance, a student who tends to talk incessantly and not stay on task can be seated at a separate table or a location away from other students.

Another possible technique for managing students while they are on computers is making laminated cards, with green on one side and red on the other, and placing the cards in cardholders on each computer monitor. The green card stays in place as long as the student is working successfully; however, when a student needs assistance from library personnel he flips over the card. A red card indicates to the library staff that the student needs some help. This unobtrusive method is especially useful with elementary students, as it is easy to understand and makes it possible for students to continue to work on task until a staff member is able to provide the needed assistance.

In the following library setting there are not enough computers for each child to have an individual computer so the librarian has developed a technique to manage the students as they share computers:

Ms. Howard, the librarian at Millard Fillmore Elementary School, assigns student partners whenever the classes work on lessons that involve computers. Once the students begin working on a lesson, it becomes very difficult to regain their attention, as the students usually talk while using the computers. When Ms. Howard needs to gain the students' attention to make an announcement or to end a lesson, she says in a firm, but not too loud voice, "Hands up!" All the children quickly place their hands in the air and face the librarian. This not only diverts their attention away from the computers, but also gives the students something to do with their hands. Many of the children look at the other students, and some strive to reach higher than their friends across the room, making it something of a competition. As soon as Ms. Howard sees all hands in the air, she then makes her announcement, without worrying that students are clicking or typing instead of listening to her.

WORKING WITH TEACHERS AND SUPPORT STAFF

The No Child Left Behind (NCLB) Act requires that every child be technology literate at the end of 8th grade (Anderson 15). As technology use becomes increasingly integrated into day-to-day learning, everyone in a school must learn how to use it. It is not possible for one school librarian to teach all the information literacy skills that are needed by all students in a school. This must be done in collaborative efforts by school librarians, teachers, and support staff.

Information technology is an ideal in-service topic for teachers and support staff. A school librarian should take an active lead in planning and implementing such professional development opportunities. After teachers have received the training needed to teach information literacy skills, school librarians and teachers can then collaboratively plan and implement lessons that use technology to educate students. In this way, all students in a school can learn to effectively and safely use the Internet, as well as the other technologies that make up the world of today's students. However, access to technology is more than just finding information; it also is about encouraging students to produce information and offering students opportunities for engaged, active learning (Anderson 18).

The knowledge and use of technology also calls attention to the role of the school librarian and broadens the librarian's sphere of influence in the school. Having technology skills and knowing how to effectively teach them to students and teachers makes the role of the school librarian indispensable. This role is more than knowing the hardware and software, but it is also about being a leader and knowing how to manage information technology. Because technology has become such a vital part of school libraries, librarians have become leaders in information technology, at both school and district levels (Brewer and Milam 50).

SUMMARY

Federal officials have talked at length about the importance of technology in the 21st century. Technology has changed the nature of learning and has profound implications for educators. Since a large portion of students' education is spent using technology, it is essential that school librarians have knowledge of how to effectively manage students as they utilize various technologies. In addition to using some helpful student management techniques, school librarians should make certain that acceptable use policies are in place so there is guidance available regarding the use of Internet by students. Librarians need to work with teachers and support staff to effectively teach information technology skills to all students, including lessons relating to Internet safety and appropriate behavior on school networks.

SCENARIOS

Think about or discuss how you could handle the following situations:

1. You are a school librarian in an elementary school that has just added a computer lab in a room adjacent the library. You have a part-time clerk in the mornings but do not know how you can manage fixed classes and a computer lab in the afternoons. Make a list of possible suggestions that you can take to your principal.
2. You are a school librarian in a middle school that has recently received 20 laptop computers that can be used for lessons in the library. Write some plans and procedures that you can use to efficiently manage students as they utilize the computers.
3. The teachers in your high school have complained that some students may be utilizing papers copied from Internet sites that provide research papers for fees. The teachers have asked you, as the librarian, to help them address this problem. What are some of the things that you might do to help solve the problem?

CHAPTER 8

Library Design and Environment

Create a library environment that is welcoming.

Creating a library environment that is warm and friendly can contribute to good management of students. When young people feel they are welcomed into the library, they are more apt to respect library personnel and facilities. A simple smile from a school librarian can go a long way in attracting users and making them feel comfortable in the library.

As the enrollment of students with special needs increases in public schools, school officials must also consider how to accommodate the needs of these students as they utilize the library facilities. All students deserve equitable access to information in an environment that is both safe and conducive to learning; school librarians need to be proactive in helping ensure that this occurs in their facilities.

The design and layout of the library can serve as an ounce of prevention when trying to create an environment that is contributes to good classroom management. Design needs may change, along with other aspects of society. Technology has greatly affected the layouts of libraries and most likely will continue to do so. Therefore, flexibility in design is essential.

OVERALL ENVIRONMENT

Providing a pleasant environment can help librarians manage the students who use school libraries. An appropriate attitude and sincerity of all library personnel to serve the needs and interests of students improves a library program. Knowledge of disability legislation and taking into consideration the feelings and perspectives of students with disabilities can help create an ideal environment for a school library. A poor attitude and approach to library services, on the other hand, can discourage students from using the library and can contribute to misbehavior of those students who do use the library.

Regularly displaying student artwork or other projects helps students realize that school librarians are interested in them as individuals. Students can also be asked to share their special collections in glass display cases.

> Mr. Dodd has created a library that is welcoming and child-centered at Riverview Elementary Charter School. He has procedures in place that the children are familiar with and routinely follow. Every student entering the library knows exactly what is expected. He has developed activities that are interesting to the students, and he generates excitement with his library lessons. He treats every child with respect. When a child acts out, he pulls the child aside and speaks softly to the student. He never yells or speaks disrespectfully. Mr. Dodd is also passionate about books and wants that passion to be contagious. He frequently displays in the library student artwork relating to the books that children read.

FACILITY DESIGN AND LAYOUT

One of the most critical factors to consider in the layout of a library is to make certain that students can be supervised from one single spot. This is especially important when a librarian is the only adult present in the library. Some states have laws requiring that students be supervised at all times in public schools. Educators who work in middle and high schools understand this is not only for safety purposes, but also for good management of students. There should be no dead zones where students can sit or hide unobserved. Placing computer screens so they can be seen by supervising library personnel is also essential for monitoring student behavior.

> When Miss Logan first visited the high school library where she was going to be doing her student teaching, Mr. Harris, the school librarian, took her on a tour of the library. He then asked her, "What do you think is wrong with the design of this library?" Miss Logan was able to note that there were some tall book stacks that prevented her from being able to see all the students. "Yes," said Mr. Harris, "unfortunately those stacks are permanent and cannot be moved. There

is not one place where I can see all of the students at the same time. When I first came here, I found that there were some students who would hit or harass other students when they were behind those high stacks. Thus, now I must spend much time moving about the library to make certain all students are supervised." He then went on to explain that the large, cumbersome circulation desk faces the front door so if he is at the circulation desk, his back is to most of the students using the library. "That is why I have our library clerk or student volunteers work the circulation desk," he stated. "I have found that it is essential to always have good visibility of the students."

If they are able to have input into an architect's design of a school library, librarians can contribute many good ideas. One consideration for increasing lines of sight is to put glass in the walls of the library office, as well as in any other rooms where students might gather. For instance, some school libraries have student group study rooms or places where students can view multimedia. If working in a library that is already built, then a librarian may need to use the types of mirrors mounted high on a wall that allow one to see around corners into areas that are not in view from the circulation desk or office.

Another concern when planning a new facility is to place tall shelves along perimeter walls, and shorter shelves in the middle part of the room. In such a layout, visibility is increased. It is also wise to purchase shorter shelves and display cases that are on wheels and are moveable. This makes it possible not only to place shelves where visibility is not hampered, but to also to use the space for a variety of purposes.

The Marshall Middle School Library was recently remodeled. The permanent shelves that sat at one end and in the middle of the library were replaced with several sections of low moveable shelves. When a storyteller came for a visit, all four sixth grades were invited into the library. In five minutes, the librarian and her library clerk moved the low shelves to three sides of the room, and the sixth grade classes entered the library one at a time with their teachers. All the students sat on the floor and listened attentively for 50 minutes while the storyteller shared several stories and talked about the art of storytelling. During the storytelling program, a few individual students from other classes were able to unobtrusively use the section of the library close to the entrance where class tables are in place. At the end of the period, the shelves were quickly moved back, and the regular library scheduling resumed.

There are numerous other design considerations that help classroom management in a school library. Some such factors include the
following:

- Locating the library away from noisy areas, such as cafeterias and
  gymnasiums
- Placing the circulation area, library office, and workroom near
  the library entrance
- Locating an equipment or teacher workroom with an exit to the
  corridor
- Providing low shelving for picture books next to the story time
  area
- Having temperature controls accessible to only authorized per-
  sonnel
- Planning for bulletin boards and display cases where students
  will be able to easily see them
- Planning ahead for the accommodations of new technologies
- Making certain that furnishings and décor are age appropriate
- Purchasing stackable chairs that can be easily moved
- Providing space for a copy machine
- Locating a security system near the library exit in high school li-
  braries
- Including an outside wall that can be opened if the need for more
  space occurs

Organizing space in the library can have an impact on students'
behavior. Having students not face potential sources of distraction,
such as windows or doors, creates fewer behavior problems. This is
especially true for younger children. Thus, it is wise to have a library
storytime in an area that is away from the circulation desk and any en-
trances to the library. A librarian can place the chair in which he plans
to sit in front of a wall or bookshelves, and have students face him.

Library furniture and shelves should be placed so that pathways
facilitate traffic flow. The needs of students in wheelchairs also should
be considered. The Americans with Disabilities Act (ADA) requires at
least 36 inches between library bookshelf units to make them accessible to wheelchair patrons. Placing bookshelf units 42 inches apart
makes it possible for such patrons to turn around in the aisles and
face materials on the opposite shelves. Heavily used items should
be located on lower shelves, where they can easily be reached by all
students.

Other facility considerations for meeting the needs of students with
disabilities include:

- The entrance to the library should be easily accessible to students who are physically challenged. A large electric button should be at wheelchair level to open automatic doors.
- All doors in the library should swing in the same direction.
- Door levers that can be pushed down are easier to open than doorknobs that need to be turned.
- No changes of floor levels should be included in the design.
- Ideally, a school library should be placed on the ground floor. If it is located on a higher floor, elevator access must be provided.
- If a security system is in place, it should be barrier free and not have turnstiles.
- Obstacles should be kept off the floor. This includes raised electric outlet covers.
- The library furniture should be arranged in an organized manner and be clutter-free.
- Tables should be sturdy and high enough for wheelchair arms to fit under.
- Some computer stations need to be at levels where students in wheelchairs can work comfortably.
- Assistive technologies should be used to facilitate access to learning opportunities for students with disabilities.

If helping design a new library, school librarians should consider carefully whether to include restrooms that are accessible to students. Although it may be handy to have a restroom in an elementary school library when kindergarten students need to use the facilities during story hours, having a student bathroom for middle school and high school students will most likely present some possible problems. If there are not two adults of opposite sex working in the library at all times, monitoring a student restroom may be very difficult if inappropriate behavior is suspected. The placement of a restroom in an area accessible by only library staff, however, can be extremely helpful, and the restroom can be used for student emergencies, with staff consent.

Proper acoustics and lighting can also assist in effectively managing students. Floor layout and coverings affect the acoustics of a facility, as do ceiling and wall coverings. Carpeting generally can improve the acoustics of a room for students with hearing disabilities, yet at the same time may make it more difficult for students in wheelchairs to move about the library. If helping design a library, some professional assistance in planning the acoustics might be needed. This is also true of lighting. Glare-free lighting is important, and shades or blinds should be provided for windows. Skylights should be avoided.

When Mrs. Knight took the position of librarian at Oakwood High School, she was pleased to see that the library had a large skylight that let in the Florida sunlight and kept the area bright and cheerful. The library itself was very sizeable, with a capacity seating of more than 100 students. The facility was divided into three sections by low bookshelves, so she could easily plan to have at least two classes in the library at one time, with tables in two sections, plus leave a leisure reading section with a few tables and some comfortable, casual chairs for other students coming to use the facility. She was also able to view all students using the library from the glassed-in library office. There was a single large room in each corner of the library—the office in one corner near the entrance, an equipment storage room in another corner, a magazine area and copy machine in a third corner, and a library and teacher workroom in the last corner. The library itself was extremely attractive with sunshine yellow walls, orange counter tops, and a relatively new carpet with orange and yellow flecks.

However, Mrs. Knight soon realized that there were some major problems with the library facilities. When classes and teachers began to use the library, she found that she spent a good deal of the day traveling back and forth to the four rooms in the corners of the library to retrieve needed items. By the end of the day, she was exhausted. Then, when a class came in to use the middle section of the library, which sits under the large skylight, she discovered that because of the sun coming down through the skylight, she was unable to adequately project her planned lesson onto a screen so the students could see it. With numerous days of sunshine in Florida, that area of the library became unusable for many class lessons.

When a new teacher who used a wheelchair was hired the next year, and became a frequent library user, Mrs. Knight found that she needed to keep constant watch to open the large, heavy glass entrance doors for him. Then, at the end of that year, the assistant principal announced that the entire inside of the school was scheduled to be repainted, and it had been decided by the administration that all rooms would be painted either mauve or gray, so an attractive color scheme could be carried out throughout the school. Mrs. Knight immediately began to picture how awful the orange counters and yellow and orange carpeting would look with mauve walls. A wave of depression overcame her as she faced the reality that she might need to look at gray walls all day long.

In the above example, it is easy to see that an aesthetically pleasing library facility, although desirable, is not enough to meet student and teacher needs. In many instances, librarians need to work within the confines of an existing facility. However, whenever a new school is being built or a library is being remodeled, it is essential that a school librarian be proactive in the planning of the library facility.

There are, however, things that librarians can physically do with existing facilities to more effectively manage students. Furniture can be rearranged. For instance, a circulation desk can be changed to face a student area, rather than an exit. In a high school library, a librarian desk can be placed in front of a classroom area so the librarian is always available for assistance, rather than working away from students in a library office. Sections of the library can be created so that there are quiet areas for research located near the reference resources and computers. Furniture and sections of the library can be arranged so that students and teachers walking into the library can walk to different areas without disturbing others.

When students can listen and follow instructions without moving from the places where they are seated, there are also apt to be fewer problems than when students have to get up and move around. Thus, librarians can make certain that all chairs and tables that are needed for a class are in place before students enter for an activity. Librarians should also ask students to tuck chairs under the tables when not in use or at the end of a class period so there are open walkways throughout the library.

Adding high visibility signage that is large and clear will help students more easily find materials and work independently. Signs with raised letters or Braille symbols are ideal for meeting the needs of visually impaired students. Flashing lights for fire alarms help hearing impaired students, and the management and safety of all students can be aided by practicing emergency drills in the library.

SUMMARY

The design and furnishing of a school library can affect management of students at all school levels. In elementary schools, storytime areas should be located in a place away from distractions and noise. Secondary schools that are flexibly scheduled should have sections of the library set aside where classes can meet separately, and other students and teachers can use the library without disturbing classes. All school librarians must consider the needs of students with disabilities—keeping pathways clear of obstructions, providing sturdy furniture at appropriate levels, and placing bookshelves far enough apart for students in wheelchairs to easily maneuver through aisles to retrieve materials. One of the most essential considerations in designing a library is to make certain that all students are in view from the librarian's primary supervisory location. A welcoming, pleasant atmosphere also attracts students to a library and helps maintain appropriate student behavior.

SCENARIOS

Complete the activities for the following situations:

1. You have been hired to be the librarian for a new elementary school that is being built. Make a list of some of the items that you would like the architect to consider when he designs the new school library.
2. You have been given some funds to refurnish an older high school library in which you are the librarian. Select some furniture from library catalogs that you would like to purchase. Remember to include considerations for the special need students who use the library.
3. You are the librarian in a middle school in which it has been difficult to effectively manage student behavior. The principal has informed you that the library is scheduled to be renovated. Make a layout for the library that you think could improve the management of students.

Works Cited

Anderson, Mary Alice. "Technician or Technologist? Technology and the Role of the Library Media Specialist." *Library Media Connection* 24.1 (2005): 14–16, 18, 109.

Barnard, Madelene Rathbun. "Sticks, Stones, and Words Can Hurt You: Antibullying Resources." *Young Adult Library Services* 8.1 (2009): 33–39.

Boynton, Mark, and Christine Boynton. *The Educator's Guide to Preventing and Solving Discipline Problems.* Alexandria, VA: Association for Supervision and Curriculum Development, 2005.

Brewer, Peggy, and Peggy Milam. "SLJ's Technology Survey 2006." *School Library Journal* 2.6 (2006): 46–50.

Bullying Statistics. "Bullying Statistics 2009." 2009. <http://www.bullyingstatistics.org/content/bullying-statistics-2009.html>

Bullying.org. "Where You Are Not Alone." Undated. <http://www.bullying.org>

Curwin, Richard L., and Allen N. Mendler. *Discipline with Dignity.* Alexandria, VA: Association for Supervision and Curriculum Development, 1988.

Curwin, Richard L., Allen N. Mendler, and Brian D. Mendler. *Discipline with Dignity.* 3rd ed. Alexandria, VA: Association for Supervision and Curriculum Development, 2008.

Flicker, Eileen S., and Janet Andron Hoffman. *Guiding Children's Behavior: Developmental Discipline in the Classroom.* New York: Teachers College, Columbia University, 2006.

GLSEN. "2007 National School Climate Survey: Nearly 9 out of 10 LGBT Students Harassed." 2008. <http://www.glsen.org/cgi-bin/iowa/all/library/record/2340.html>

Gootman, Marilyn E. *The Caring Teacher's Guide to Discipline: Helping Students Learn Self-Control, Responsibility, and Respect, K-6.* 3rd ed. Thousand Oaks, CA: Corwin Press, 2008.

Hardman, Michael L., and Shirley Dawson. "The Impact of Federal Public Policy on Curriculum and Instruction for Students with Disabilities in the General Classroom." *Preventing School Failure* 52.2 (2008): 5–11.

Hopkins, Janet. "Extending Inclusive Learning: Library and Special Educa-
    tion Collaboration." *Library Media Connection* 23.6 (2005): 17–19.

Logsdon, Ann. "Least Restrictive Environment—What Is the Least Restrictive
    Environment?" Undated. <http://learningdisabilities.about.com/od/
    publicschoolprograms/a/leastrestrictiv.htm>

Martin, Betty. "Interpersonal Relations and the School Library Media Special-
    ist." *School Library Media Quarterly* 11.1 (1982): 43–44, 53–57.

Marzano, Robert J., Jana S. Marzano, and Debora Pickering. *Classroom Manage-
    ment That Works: Research-based Strategies for Every Teacher.* Alexandria,
    VA: Association for Supervision and Curriculum Development, 2003.

Murray, Janet. "Teaching Information Skills to Students with Disabilities:
    What Works?" *School Libraries Worldwide* 7.2 (2001): 1–16.

National Association for Homeless Education at the SERVE Center.
    "McKinney-Vento." Undated. <http://www.terrifictransitions.org/nche/
    m-v.php>

New York Times. "Diversity in the Classroom." Undated. <http://projects.ny
    times.com/immigration/enrollment>

Nichols, Beverly. *Improving Student Achievement: 50 More Research-Based
    Strategies for Educators.* Columbus, OH: Linworth, 2009.

North American Montessori Center. "Montessori Panes of Development:
    Upper Elementary Characteristics." 6 Jan. 2010. <http://montessori
    training.blogspot.com/2010/01/montessori-planes-of-development-
    upper.html>

Pennington, Mark. "Characteristics of High School Learners." 2 Nov. 2008.
    <http://ezinearticles.com/?Characteristics-of-High-School-Learners&
    id=1641532>

Scarlett, W. George, Iris Chin Ponte, and Jay P. Singh. *Approaches to Behavior
    and Classroom Management: Integrating Discipline and Care.* Los Angeles:
    Sage, 2009.

Schipman, Mavis. "It's Cool to Work in the Library . . . Student Library Aides."
    Library Media Connection 25.3 (2006): 26–27.

Shaw, Carla Cooper. "Critical Issue: Educating Teachers for Diversity." 1997.
    <http://www.ncrel.org/sdrs/areas/issues/educatrs/presrvce/pe300.
    htm>

Thomas, Nancy. "Teaching 'Kids,' Not 'Content': Recreating the School Library
    Media Center as a Caring Context for Student Learning." *School Library
    Media Activities Monthly* 17.2 (2000): 23–24, 39, 48.

Walker, Hill M., Elizabeth Ramsey, and Frank M. Gresham. "Heading Off Dis-
    ruptive Behavior." *American Educator* 27.4 (2003/04): 6–15.

Index

Acceptable use policies (AUPs), 79–81, 84
Acoustics, 91
ADA. *See* Americans with Disabilities Act
ADHD. *See* Attention deficit hyperactivity disorders
Americans with Disabilities Act (ADA), 66, 90
Asperger's syndrome, 68, 75
Assistive technologies, 71, 91
Attention deficit hyperactivity disorders (ADHD), 70, 71
AUP. *See* Acceptable use policies
Autism, 65, 68, 75

Bullying, 5, 6; high school, 58–60, 64; middle school, 42–44, 50; students from diverse backgrounds, 69–70, 74

Checkout, 10, 14, 20, 21
Chinese American students, 67
Class activities, 44, 60, 70, 81
Collaboration, 23, 40, 52, 73, 74
Computer lab, 77, 78, 79, 82, 85
Consequences, 5; high school, 57, 58, 62, 63; middle school, 45; students from diverse backgrounds, 69; violating the acceptable use policy, 80
Contracts, 5, 7, 34–35

Copy machine, 90, 92
Correcting behavior, 4, 5
Cyber bullying, 6, 43, 70

Disabilities: American with Disabilities Act, 66, 90; bullying, 43, 69; library design and environment, 88, 90, 91, 94; students from diverse backgrounds, 65, 72
Discipline, 1, 2, 5–6; high school, 57, 58, 63, 64; middle school, 40, 42, 46, 50; record, 58–59; upper elementary school, 37
Diverse backgrounds, 60, 65–74

Effective communication, 40, 54, 67, 78
ELLs. *See* English language learners
English as a second language (ESL), 73
English language learners (ELLs), 65, 68, 69, 72
ESL. *See* English as a second language
Expectations, 2, 3; acceptable use policy, 79; high school, 62; lower elementary school, 11; middle school, 47; upper elementary school, 30, 34, 37

Facility design, 87–94
Fighting, 62, 70
Fixed scheduling, 10, 28, 36

Flexible scheduling: high school, 52, 63; lower elementary school, 10; middle school, 40, 47, 49, 50; upper elementary school, 28, 36
Following up, 6–7
Furniture, 56, 90, 91, 93, 94

Gaining attention, 10, 19, 28, 32, 39
Games, 18, 33, 42

High school students, 2, 4, 7, 29, 43, 51–64, 91
Humor, 27, 40, 41, 50, 55, 60

IDEA. *See* Individuals with Disabilities Education Act
IEPs. *See* Individual educational programs
Inclusion, 69
Individual educational programs (IEPs), 34, 36, 66, 71, 74
Individuals with Disabilities Education Act (IDEA), 66
Internet safety, 78, 84
Interruptions, 17, 45

Japanese American students, 67

Lesson plans, 36, 47, 48
Library design. *See* Facility design
Library environment, 1, 3, 4; design, 87–94; high school, 54, 64; lower elementary school, 18, 19, 23, 24; upper elementary school, 27, 29
Library orientations, 21, 42, 43, 47, 56, 57, 71
Library privileges, 7, 35, 57, 79, 80
Lighting, 91
Lower elementary students, 9–25

McKinney-Vento Homeless Assistance Act, 66, 67
Mexican American students, 67
Middle school students, 39–50; first class visit, 2; Internet use, 80; library design, 89, 91, 94; students from diverse backgrounds, 74, 75
Music, 20

Native American students, 49, 56, 66, 67, 69
NCLB. *See* No Child Left Behind Act
No Child Left Behind Act (NCLB), 58, 66, 67, 83
Nonverbal messages, 41, 60, 67, 68

Parents, 6; acceptable use policy, 80; lower elementary school, 20, 23–24; middle school, 49; students from diverse backgrounds, 70, 73; upper elementary school, 34, 36–37
Positive relationships, 24, 36, 39, 40
Power struggles, 5, 46, 61
Praise, 3, 23, 31, 32, 55
Problem students, 21, 28, 33, 34, 45, 46, 61, 73
Proximity, 4, 41

Respect, 1, 4; high school, 54, 55, 56, 63; library environment and design, 87, 88; middle school, 39, 41, 50; students from diverse backgrounds, 67, 68, 69, 70, 74
Rewards, 22, 23, 35, 36
Routines, 3, 14, 15, 20, 31, 54

Safety, 70, 78, 80, 84, 88, 93
Scenarios, 25, 38, 50, 64, 74, 85, 94
Scheduling. *See* Fixed scheduling; Flexible scheduling
School-wide policies and programs, 4, 81
Seating, 4, 16, 17, 18, 28, 30, 83
Security systems, 62, 90, 91
Sexual orientation, 43, 61, 69, 73
Shelving, 47, 63, 90
Signage, 14, 93
Special needs, 65–74, 87
Storytime, 4, 6, 11; gaining and keeping attention, 10–13; library design, 90, 93; problem children,

21; routine, 14; scenario, 25; scheduling, 10, 11; story selection, 23; techniques, 15–17; transitions, 19, 20

Supervision, 6, 58, 77

Support staff: high school, 62; lower elementary school, 12, 14, 23; middle school, 47, 49; students with diverse backgrounds, 71, 73–74; technology, 83–84; upper elementary school, 28, 36–37

Table activities, 14, 17, 23, 30

Technology, 77–85, 87

Theft, 62, 78

Time-out, 4, 6, 21, 46, 62, 71

Transitions, 10, 19, 20, 24, 29, 32

Upper elementary students, 27–38

Visibility, 16, 89, 93

Volunteers, 3, 89; high school, 63; lower elementary school, 14, 20, 23; middle school, 46, 49; students from diverse backgrounds, 75; upper elementary school, 37, 46

Wheelchair access, 68, 90, 91, 92, 94

About the Authors

KAY BISHOP is an associate professor at the State University of New York at Buffalo, where she has served as Director of the School Library Media Program and Director of the Online MLS Program. She has also been on the faculty at the University of South Florida, the University of Kentucky, the University of Southern Mississippi, and Murray State University. Kay has more than 20 years of experience as a school librarian at various grade levels. She is the author of numerous articles, chapters in books, and two other books: *Connecting Libraries with Classrooms: The Curricular Roles of the Media Specialist*, 2nd edition (Linworth, 2011) and *The Collection Program in Schools: Concepts, Practices, and Information Sources*, 4th edition (Libraries Unlimited, 2007). Additionally, Kay has coauthored the following books: *Staff Development Guide to Workshops for Technology and Information Literacy: Ready to Present* (Linworth, 2005) and *Inquiry-Based Learning: Lessons from Library Power* (Linworth, 2001).

JENNY CAHALL is an instructional designer for a K–12 educational company in Victor, NY. She has been involved in writing, reviewing, and editing educational products for the past 12 years. She especially enjoys developing science curriculum and sharing her love of learning with her children, Adam and Megan.

Made in the USA
Lexington, KY
26 August 2012